A BUSINESS BUILT TO LAST

A memoir of finance, family and fun

JOHN HEWISON

First published 2025

Text © John Hewison 2025
Design and typography © 2025

Edited by Holly Proctor
Text design and typesetting by WorkingType Studio
Cover design by WorkingType Studio

Photographs courtesy of Hewison Private Wealth
Printed in Australia by IngramSpark

Paperback ISBN: 978-1-7637888-7-9
ePUB ISBN: 978-1-7637888-8-6

NATIONAL
LIBRARY
OF AUSTRALIA

A catalogue record for this
book is available from the
National Library of Australia

Disclaimer: The material in this publication is of the nature of general comment only and does
not represent professional advice. It is not intended to provide specific guidance for particular
circumstances, and it should not be relied on as the basis for any decision to take action or not
take action on any matter which it covers. Readers should obtain professional advice where
appropriate, before making any such decision. To the maximum extent permitted by law, the
author disclaims all responsibility and liability to any person, arising directly or indirectly from
any person taking or not taking action based on the information in this publication.

*To my wife, Helen, for her love, support, partnership and trust.
And to our children, Sarah and Andrew, for their love, friendship
and support when I needed it most.*

Contents

Preface

Hewison Private Wealth (HPW) is an independently owned, financial advisory and portfolio management business established by me as founder in 1985 with the support of my wife, Helen. Over four decades, the business has flourished to become a dynamic and extraordinarily successful organisation providing bespoke financial advice and managing more than $2 billion of private clients' funds. Whilst that is the technical basis of what HPW does, what we do and how we do it, and the things that have made the business phenomenally successful, is a different and unique story.

From the start of this journey, I had a set of core beliefs and philosophies that I had developed through my personal standards and business experiences that would help shape the business. Over the years, our team would grow to not just adopt these standards but embrace them, live them and take ownership of them. The result was astounding. How we engendered buy-in, universal commitment and ownership of these core beliefs formed the basis of a culture that had to be seen to be believed and was the key element of our success. The initiatives we took were the key drivers to achieving this extraordinary cultural phenomenon, together with the quality of the individuals who formed our team.

I never considered myself an entrepreneur in the strict sense of the word, but I had always had a drive to succeed in all that I did and a passion for innovation and looking for new and better ways to do things. I am a 'conservative' risk-taker – that is, I thrive on taking risks to try something new, but I am always cautious to think things through, then consider and manage the downside if things do not work out. I guess you could call it taking a risk with a safety net.

Our story is about our successes, but throughout the journey we encountered several challenges, some of which had the potential to destroy us. How we survived and reacted to these challenges is an important part of our story, which not only tested our philosophies but made us stronger and more committed to them than ever. Over the years, we have always viewed challenges as being test cases and made sure that we learnt and reacted accordingly by being open to adapting to inevitable change. This has been another key to our success.

Whilst this book is about structure and culture, we were in the business of investing clients' money, achieving results and protecting their financial wellbeing. Our innovation and creativity also extended into our investment philosophy, which included investment policy, systemic processes and disciplined portfolio management practices. Whilst this is not intended to be a book about investment per se, it is an important part of our innovative philosophies and had to be included.

As I finally step into retirement from the business, my overwhelming feelings are of absolute excitement for the future of the business and all who are associated with it. I have enormous pride, joy and satisfaction in the realisation that we have achieved all the original core beliefs upon which the business was based and that those lofty goals remain the focus of the business as it continues to thrive in the hands of my younger protégés. But what that model has become is something I could never have anticipated and is beyond my wildest dreams.

My motivation in authoring this book is to share the extraordinary successes we achieved, developing from a sole trader start-up into a fully corporatised and sustainable business with a stable recurrent revenue base and a consistent, continuing growth record. But more importantly, is the heart and soul of a phenomenon built on close relationships, both internal and external, and a set of core values that were non-negotiable and have stood the test of time. We have succeeded in building a model of excellence with a big heart.

When I look back through my business career, I was fortunate to have achieved success through my time in the corporate sector, which eventually set me up to establish my own business. As a businessperson and a professional, I achieved a level of success I could never have anticipated, on many levels, and which I still find difficult to believe. This is a story of how we had the foresight and courage to use groundbreaking strategies, philosophies and innovations that stood us apart from our competitors. It also helped us to achieve a level of excellence and success that no doubt enabled us to not just survive but to achieve great outcomes. It was about the standards we set, the unorthodox initiatives we undertook and the culture we built, all of which enabled us to achieve a level of success that I could never have anticipated in my wildest dreams. It is about how we survived and the beliefs, standards, systems and processes that saved us and allowed us to flourish in the face of adversity. I look back and wonder how we could have reached the dizzy heights of success that we did, despite encountering extreme hazards along the way. It constantly blows my mind.

The business model we created is universally applicable to all businesses, but as we were in the business of providing professional financial planning advice, investment advice and ongoing client management, the methodologies, principles and disciplines we created were vital factors to success. Whilst specialised in some ways, the principles we employed apply to any business.

There are two main parts to my story: 'The journey' and 'My core beliefs', with the part, 'Achieving outcomes' concluding the book.

Part 1, 'The journey' (covered in detail in chapters 1–10), is the warts and all experience of building a successful business; the triumphs, the challenges and the heartbreaks, which at times almost brought me to my knees. The overriding messages focus on secrets to our success that enabled us to survive and thrive. The general principles we applied are the things that are universally applicable to any business.

Part 2, 'My core beliefs' (covered in detail in chapters 11–18), refers to the non-negotiable set of standards I aimed to achieve and the philosophies that grew from those standards, which determined us as an organisation and became part of our culture. These core beliefs are about the mission and the outcomes I wanted to achieve in the long term, and these formed the basis of our business plan.

Part 3, 'Achieving outcomes' (covered in chapters 19–20), is the concluding section that looks at the broader picture of the profession both in Australia and internationally, and the role I played. Finally, it discusses how we sum up Hewison Private Wealth in four key words and concludes with me handing over the reins of the business to my colleagues and the transition to the next phase into the future.

About the author

I am a baby boomer, born in 1947 to a middle-class Melbourne family. I left school at the age of 16 after completing Year 11 and achieving the entry standard for the Australian Society of Accountants (now CPA Australia) study program. I got a clerical job as an accounting trainee with a shipping company and studied accountancy part-time.

At 19 years of age, I was bored and wanted to do something more creative and exciting. Also, my employer had provided me with a road map of my future career path, which was less than inspiring, so I left and moved to a role in an advertising agency, which was an exciting change of pace. From there I moved into the world of sales and marketing. I enjoyed success in several roles in varying industries, which all resulted from clients poaching me to work for them. In 1974, I was offered a position with a division of the Australian Stock Exchange (ASX)-listed company Brash Holdings Ltd (Brash), initially to set up a Queensland branch for their wholesale division Australian Musical Industries (AMI), which imported and marketed home entertainment products including audio systems and TVs. I created an extraordinarily successful distribution branch and was then transferred back to Melbourne head office, where I was to progress through senior management positions over the next 10 years. This gave me a solid basis and experience of management expertise, both good and bad, and so I began to develop my core standards and beliefs.

It was around this time that I read Robert Townsend's celebrated book *Up the Organisation*, which was radical for its time and formulated my core beliefs around flat management structures and empowerment of the individual. I successfully put these theories into practice during my corporate experience, and this was a key part of my set of core management beliefs, which I will discuss in greater detail later.

I resigned from corporate management in 1983 at the age of 36, having tired of corporate politics and constant travelling, which kept me away from my wife and young children for extended periods of time. I had applied for a less demanding corporate position but was shocked to learn from a management consultant that I had been previously paid in the top 1% of salary earners. I knew I was well paid but was by no means living the dream and still had a healthy mortgage. It was then that I decided there had to be a better way; I had to build my own business.

I discussed the prospect of going it alone with my wife, Helen, who, to my surprise and her absolute credit, supported the idea of setting up a business and using my superannuation and Brash shares, which I had accumulated via an employee share scheme, to fund the venture. I established a marketing and business consulting company through which, initially, my former employers contracted my services, as did a New Zealand-based counterpart. I also consulted for a family business, which led to a sideline in landscape design for which I completed a diploma and established a swimming pool solar heating business.

I had plenty of work, which was financially rewarding, and it was great having the flexibility to spend time with my young family. Unfortunately, however, it was not the sort of business that had the potential to grow into something more substantial or offer ongoing financial security.

In 1985, I became interested in the emerging profession of financial planning through an acquaintance by the name of Michael Wilson, who was one of the principals of financial advice firm Beyson Investment Services (Beyson).

Following the reform and deregulation of the Australian financial system in the early 1980s, there was huge growth in the public need for financial advice. My background in accountancy, marketing and broad business management roles in various industries all combined to prepare me well for this opportunity. I liked the idea of developing a professional career in an area of creativity and excitement and caring for people's financial wellbeing.

I obtained a securities dealer representative licence and established a financial planning business, Hewison & Associates Pty Ltd, firstly as an authorised representative of Beyson. Later, I obtained a securities dealer licence and operated independently under the name Hewison Private Wealth, which still endures today.

From the outset, I was always innovative and creative by nature and tried to stay ahead of the pack. I employed new initiatives and unconventional methods, and as we developed, we were always considered agents of change. Invariably, our initiatives were proven to be successful, but no-one is perfect and we made mistakes along the way, as you will find out. I am very much of the mindset that it is better to have a crack at something new and get it wrong rather than doing nothing and just remaining like everyone else. Daring to be different and creating a better client outcome is one of the major keys to success.

As I write this, the business continues its successful operation and continuous growth and has a business model that is solid and sustainable with minimal risk. I am now recently retired and satisfied that the business is well cared for, with solid relationships and a business plan, philosophy and culture that will enable it to continue to thrive into the future. But more importantly than fundamental, I sit back and marvel at this phenomenal living thing that we have created. The people, the culture, the relationships, the absolute commitment to excellence in everything and the caring. It is just unbelievable.

I still get goose bumps when I think of the initiatives we took, the innovations we pioneered and the disasters we survived. But, most importantly, I remain in awe of the extraordinary outcomes we achieved throughout our journey.

Above all, the business and its philosophies continue to flourish beyond me – truly a business built to last.

Acknowledgements

The production of this book would not have been possible without the support, advice and guidance provided initially by Lou Johnson who reviewed the early draft. She challenged me to focus on the core subject and determine the 'what' and the 'why' — key considerations in writing this story. Lou then referred me to Debbie Lee, an independent publishing consultant who undertook the overall management of the book's production, connecting me with appropriate people and services. To this end, I wish to thank Holly Proctor, editor and all-round content adviser, for providing me with guidance and suggestions for the layout, formatting and content of the book, as well as editing it into a much-improved version and helping me to tell my story. I cannot thank her enough. Likewise, thanks to Luke Harris of Working Type for his great work in the design and layout of the book and assisting me through the publishing process. I also acknowledge financial media stalwart and long-time industry associate Bruce Madden for connecting me with Lou and supporting the fight for lifting professional standards in the financial planning profession over many years.

I wish to acknowledge and thank the many people who partnered with me, supported me and believed in me throughout my journey, especially when the going got tough. My wonderful and loyal clients, my professional and industry colleagues, my family and my friends. I will be eternally grateful to them all.

I acknowledge my primary mentors, Geoffrey Brash and my dear friend Rob Roberts, who both helped shape my core business beliefs and values. I also acknowledge Rob's continuing role throughout my career as a trusted friend, as my business 'coach' via The Executive Connection, as a client and as our company chairman.

I could not have achieved the outcomes of my journey without the support and sharing of the dream by my business colleagues. My special thanks to my fellow team members at Hewison Private Wealth, who through their commitment and empowerment made me redundant. Whilst there are too many to name individually, I need to acknowledge the loyalty and support of Janine Gordon, without whom I would not have survived our encounter with a fraudulent partner. To my first graduate appointment and partner, Chris Morcom, for his enduring loyalty and outstanding professionalism. To my Executive Assistant for over 20 years, Clare Blizzard, for her loyalty and dedication to the business and particularly our clients. To Practice Manager, Effie Goumas, for her professionalism, friendship and loyalty, and for the great contribution she made over many years. And to my son, Andrew, for leading the business forward following my retirement and his ongoing support. I'd also like to thank my other business partners for sharing the mission and continuing the journey into the future.

My final thanks are to my wife, Helen, without whom I would not have achieved the success I did throughout my career. I'll be forever grateful for her love and support.

List of shortened forms

AFL	Australian Football League
AMI	Australian Musical Industries
ASC	Australian Securities Commission
ASIC	Australian Securities and Investments Commission
ASX	Australian Stock Exchange
ATO	Australian Tax Office
CBA	Commonwealth Bank of Australia
CBD	Central Business District
CEO	Chief Executive Officer
CFP	Certified Financial Planner
CPA	Australia – Certified Practising Accountants of Australia
CSM	Customer Success Management
FP	Financial planning
FPA	Financial Planning Association of Australia
FPSB	Financial Planning Standards Board
GFC	Global financial crisis
HPW	Hewison Private Wealth
IMA	Individually Managed Account
IT	Information technology
NCSC	National Companies and Securities Commission
PA	Portfolio Administration
PA	Personal assistant
PI	Professional indemnity
US	United States

My core beliefs: the business plan

L ike most people, I suppose, my core beliefs were developed through my childhood, business and life experiences. Like anyone, I went through different phases in life, some good, some not so good, but that is the learning experience. I credit my parents for bringing me up with basic standards of decency, honesty, fairness, accountability and a good work ethic. But the school of hard knocks taught me as well, and I derived value from recognising poor examples of behaviour as well as being inspired by the exemplary.

I was lucky to come from a business background that exposed me to great leaders and mentors who taught me principles and standards of behaviour that would serve me well. I also experienced poor behaviour too, which was essential in helping me formulate a set of behaviour values and recognise the difference in the future.

All good businesses start with a business plan. It does not need to be complex and detailed – or no-one will ever read it. But it does need to focus on the business's core beliefs and objectives.

I remember meeting one of my mentors, Geoffrey Brash, the then executive chairman of Brash Holdings and patriarch of the Brash family. I had only been with the organisation for a few days, and it was at the opening of a new service facility. Typical of Geoff, he searched me out and spent considerable time with me, asking me about myself and telling me all about the history of the Brash group.

Geoff told me how the group, which was an icon of Melbourne retail in those days, had almost gone broke earlier in the 1970s. He told me that they had strayed from their business plan and diversified into selling whitegoods at their music and home entertainment outlets. Selling low-profit, bulky goods from high-rent outlets was a disaster. He then showed me a tattered exercise book and opened to a page that simply said, 'If it doesn't make music and entertain, we don't sell it.' He said, 'That is our business plan.'

Sadly, 20 years later, after Geoff had retired, Brashs (the retail store trading name) disappeared after having diversified into books and computers; seemingly, the company had once again ventured outside their business plan.

I have never forgotten this important lesson. Thanks Geoff.

Developing the business plan

So, as we embarked on our journey into the world of financial planning, I was able to clearly articulate our core beliefs and objectives, which were focused on standards and outcomes for which I had a passionate belief. It was not about making money or achieving personal greatness; these are by-products of a successful business but not the core drivers. Do not misunderstand me; running a profitable business is essential to its success but should not be the core driver of the business plan.

My core beliefs were these:

- **Integrity and relationship values:**

  - Uphold the highest ethical standards of behaviour, honesty and fair dealing.

  - Ensure fulfilment of our fiduciary duty and maintain a 'client first' attitude in all our activities.

  - Treat everyone with respect, both internally and externally.

  - Build and maintain a reputation as a preferred business partner and always be accountable for our actions.

- **Innovation and change:**

  - Proactively and constantly look at ways to improve efficiency and outcomes.

  - Be brave and stay at the leading edge of business initiatives and relationship drivers.

  - Develop great systems and processes, particularly information technology (IT) systems development.

- **Independence and conflicts of interest:**

  - Always retain the business identity as independently owned and stay in control of our destiny.

  - Minimise the reliance on external providers, particularly with respect to our client data base, client interface, client fee for service and systemisation.

- Eliminate conflicts of interest to the extent possible with full disclosure of any unavoidable compromise.

- **People and professional standards:**

  - Build a model of professional excellence incorporating tertiary education and professional practicing standards.

  - Nurture and develop our people to ensure the maintenance of the highest standards in every respect of the profession.

  - Employ people who are smarter than me.

  - Mentor them, invest in them and provide them with the opportunity to achieve their potential, share in the company's success, and, eventually, replace me and lead the business in perpetuity.

- **Empowerment and culture:**

  - Empower those working in the business to take ownership of their role, use their initiative and take responsibility for outcomes.

  - Encourage them and provide opportunities for them to achieve their growth potential.

  - Share the dream, the mission and the passion.

  - Build a culture from a combination of commitment, mutual trust and respect into a team of empowered, like-minded individuals of mutually committed owners of the mission and the dream.

- **Corporatisation and intrinsic value:**

  - Build the business from being dependent upon a key person by hiring stars and developing them into business drivers.

  - Create a self-sustaining, mature corporate entity with systems, procedures and infrastructure.

  - Build a business model that is not transactionally driven but based on long-term client relationships and recurrent revenue streams, resulting in the company building intrinsic market value.

- **Succession: planning and implementation:**

  - Build a business to last and achieve multi-generational success beyond the founder.

  - Provide an opportunity and a mechanism for people working in the business to obtain equity ownership and implement a plan to create a smooth transition of leadership and sustain the business into the future beyond me.

  - Ensure that the business retains energy and enthusiasm and continually recreates itself through the succession process.

These were my core beliefs in 1985, and these are the core beliefs that continue to exist today. Of course, these elements all combine to develop the basis of a business's culture, which was not a commonly used term at the time, but I was to progressively learn the key importance of culture to our business.

These core beliefs are ambitious and powerful. But, I hear you say, anyone can write this stuff as window dressing – so what? Quite right, and therein lies the challenge and the key to success.

The development of culture and transition of ownership of a set of core beliefs requires courage and commitment by the business founder and those that follow. It requires a genuine ability to share ownership of the passion and also requires full disclosure, soul-baring and leadership by example. It takes courage and patience to be willing to divest power, to develop mutual trust. Say it, mean it, do it. Be willing to mentor and nurture and provide continuous encouragement and commitment. This is the hard bit, and we will talk about this in more detail later.

But the reality is that writing the business plan is one thing, implementing it and having the discipline and the commitment to live it, breathe it and own it are the real tests for all businesses.

In our business, we never stop living the plan. It is part of our DNA, and we focus on it every day in everything we do. It becomes infectious and incredibly motivational without even trying. And what is more, it is fun. How stimulating it is to come to work and mix with a diverse range of people who all take ownership and enjoy the journey that is based on standards and achieving great outcomes? An environment where everyone is on the same page and wanting to support each other to achieve positive outcomes.

Our key driver is the extremely close relationships we share with our clients, our professional colleagues and each other. But it is always referenced back to our core beliefs.

The secret is that everyone, particularly the leaders from the top down, must be proactively involved every day and lead by example with continued engagement and encouragement.

PART 1

The journey

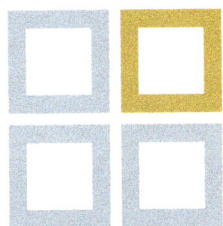

Chapter 1

The switch from accounting to sales

1966–1975

As my career progressed, in 1967 I moved into the world of commercial interior fit-outs, which eventually led me into a sales role. I was not a natural salesperson. I was quite shy and did not see myself as the selling type. The reality is that I was petrified at the thought of attempting to sell anything to anyone. One day, my boss asked me to take a furniture proposal to an existing client, a lawyer based in Melbourne's central business district (CBD). I was so nervous I couldn't stop shaking as I entered the office. Luckily for me, the receptionist was very kind and could see my panic, which she obviously passed on to her boss. He was very sympathetic and calmed me down. He also accepted the proposal I presented, and I walked out on cloud nine. My first introduction to the world of sales!

I gradually realised that marketing and sales were at the action end of any business, and that was where I wanted to be. I soon discovered, particularly in the office fit-out business, that quality salespeople based their success on delivering clever ideas and great outcomes for their clients. So, it was not about sales ability or the 'gift of the gab' as I imagined it but about the ability to discover needs and deliver outcomes that then resulted in sales.

As I progressed, I gained confidence and began to enjoy developing client relationships. I dealt with business principals and senior management and quickly learnt that those with genuine authority did not feel the need to exhibit it, whilst those who were in subordinate roles tried hard to look important. I took this on board as an important lesson for my future.

I became aware that regardless of business or profession, everyone is a salesperson. As Henry Ford was famously quoted, 'Nothing happens until someone sells something', and that is the first rule of any good business. My definition of 'selling' is developing appropriate philosophies that accommodate the establishment of good relationships, determining customer needs and providing viable solutions and outcomes; but it isn't just about the sales department. Good businesses involve all their team members in the achievement of their overall success. Every facet of a business goes to the delivery of an outcome, and every part of the process is vital. Over the years, I have seen numerous examples of divisions and jealousies forming between staff in sales, administration and supply, which destroys effective delivery.

In our business, we don't have any hierarchical divisions. Everyone is on the team to deliver, and we all celebrate our victories together. Everyone is committed to the end game of client satisfaction and going the extra mile to achieve the goal of excellence.

So, it is important to make everyone in an organisation understand that they are all part of the selling process, and no link is any more important than another.

Having achieved an important level of success in the office fit-out industry, in 1973 I was pitching for a contract to furnish a new transport terminal building for a leading express transport company by the name of Kwikasair. I had developed a great relationship with the person in charge of the project, who I later discovered was a director of the parent company. I was particularly determined to win this contract and was relentless in my pursuit. In the end, I didn't win the entire project but certainly a major portion of it in recognition of my persistence. More importantly, I was offered a job at about twice what I had been earning. I must admit, the thought of selling transport did not thrill me, but I was around 26 years of age, married and the money was too good to ignore.

I should mention that I am a fatalist by nature and believe everything happens for a reason and is in our destiny. I suspect that is why I was driven to strive for this contract, but it certainly was a serious shift in career direction for me.

Transport is tough to sell as it is not a product but a service. The opposition was plentiful and aggressive, controlled by a price-fixing cartel between the major transport companies. This meant contracts could not be won on price-cutting so had to be based on other factors such as service delivery, relationships or some other factor.

The sales training was intense and all about wordsmithing, canned presentations and jargon, none of which suited my skill set. I recall sitting through a conference watching people practising pre-scripted, canned presentations, and I thought to myself, *I could not do that in a fit.*

Based on my previous experience, I based my approach on relationship-building and problem-solving. I would call on businesses and endeavour to develop a relationship with the decision-maker or with someone who would eventually connect me to the decision-maker. This would often be the storeman or warehouse manager, with whom I would develop relationships and gather information about the transport operations and their opinions on how we might gain an advantage. These were the people who were at the coalface and could tell me where they or the company had issues.

Likewise, once I got to the decision-maker, my business experience and accounting training came in handy as I could speak their language – it was not just about selling them something.

My favourite example was a large carpet manufacturer based in Geelong. I called by one day, and rather than going to the central office, I went to the warehouse. I got talking to the warehouse manager, who often does not have anyone give him the time of day. As we got chatting, he told me that the marketing director had taken over responsibility for the company's transport. The business had suffered continuous occurrences of damage and loss of product in transit, which resulted in a major loss of interstate market share due to unreliable delivery. Bingo, that was my chance to make a difference.

I made an appointment to see the marketing director, and we talked about his issues. I discovered he was at his wits end about how to deal with this huge problem of losses and the negative impact on his interstate markets, and he was also under pressure from his board. He was sceptical about using express transport because he was aware that it was normally far too expensive for bulk goods like carpet. I suggested that I might be able to find a solution to his issues and asked him if he would consider an alternative if I could produce a viable solution to his problems. He said he would and provided me with the statistical information I needed to formulate a strategy.

I went back to my branch manager and explained the situation. He was stunned that we had the chance to win such a high-volume contract. We sat down with the terminal manager and devised a plan that would allow us to top-load carpet in space that would otherwise be vacant in the enclosed trucks we operated to transport interstate. That would enable us to price somewhere remotely within reach of general transport rates, but we would still be comparatively expensive.

I revisited my warehouse friend, took him a coffee, and brought him up to speed. He then told me that the trucking company that transported the carpets locally from Geelong to Melbourne was owned by a director of the carpet company. So, I visited him and told him what we were doing and asked him if he would continue to transport the carpet to our Melbourne terminal under our proposed new arrangement. He said he would, and he would also support our proposal if it was financially viable.

Our proposal was based around the viability of increasing transport costs but eliminating loss and damage, thus increasing interstate market share through fast, dependable and safe delivery. The marketing director was overjoyed by our proposal and took it to the board with his recommendation. We subsequently won the business.

The marketing director was excited and grateful as we had solved his biggest problem and effectively reopened his interstate markets. Kwikasair management was astounded as this was one of the biggest contracts the company had ever won, and the revenue went straight to the bottom line. I was obviously riding high on the success, but I was equally as pleased with the result we achieved for the client.

I have taken the time to tell this story as it dramatically illustrates important business principles as described here:

- Develop relationships and search for opportunities to make a difference – If I had not engaged with the warehouse manager, I never would have found out about the issues of loss and damage and the decision-maker being the marketing director.

- Always treat everyone with respect regardless, but also because you never know what knowledge they might have – The warehouse manager appreciated that I treated him with respect and sought his opinion. I had no idea he would be able to share such valuable information.

- Help to solve problems. Making sales is all about solving problems, not about convincing people to buy a product or service – I would have no hope whatsoever of landing this contract without being able to solve some serious market-related problems and provide some valuable outcomes. I provided solutions to some major problems; I did not sell the transport.

- Ask questions and listen to the answers because that is when you learn the clues to solve problems and achieve outcomes – Not only did the warehouse manager make me aware of the market-related issues, but he also told me about the local transport owner who sat on the board. With this information, I was able to assure him that we would not be taking away his business and gain his support for our proposal.

- Think creatively – I could have never competed on price in the example above, but I won the contract by thinking outside the box and responding creatively to the client's key problem issues and by value-adding.

- Always be genuine and sincere. Most people have excellent 'bullshit' meters – I won the marketing manager's confidence as I was able to show him that I genuinely cared about his dilemma and had thought through the possibility of a viable solution. If I had just tried to just 'sell' him on an alternative transport service, he would not have been interested.

Postscript

Soon after I won the carpet deal, I resigned after being offered a wonderful opportunity by one of my other transport clients. I had also learnt that two other salespeople at Kwikasair were being paid more than me but producing nowhere near my level of business. My boss immediately tried to convince me to stay by offering me more money. I just simply said, 'Sorry Max, you're too late.'

This experience taught me to make sure your people are paid based on performance, not just with respect to sales, but in all spheres of the business. Everyone in an organisation is in the relationship business and a vital cog in the wheel so deserve to be rewarded for effort and personal development. In my entire management career spanning 50 years, I have only ever had two people ask me for a salary increase. Neither was deserving, and neither became long-term employees.

Chapter 2

Learning through experience: my corporate life

1975–1983

At the age of 27, I was offered a position with Australian Musical Industries (AMI), one of my Kwikasair transport clients. AMI was the import and wholesale division of Brash Holdings. I was appointed with a view to moving to Brisbane to set up a Queensland distribution branch for the wholesale marketing of home entertainment products – audio and television, then later musical instruments. I jumped at the chance.

Shortly after joining AMI, I attended the opening of a new Brash group technical and service facility, which was located at the AMI premises. It was at this event that I met two men who would become important mentors to me: Geoffrey Brash, the executive chair of the Brash group of companies, and Rob Roberts, who had just joined the group as managing director of the musical instrument division of AMI. Rob and I hit it off right away and became incredibly good friends. Geoff was an inspirational leader and an outstanding gentleman with whom I developed a close relationship. I benefitted enormously from both of these fine men, to whom I am eternally grateful.

Having relocated to Brisbane with my wife, Helen, I set up a small office showroom, employed a personal assistant and set about building the business. It was tough work as I had to initially get over the Queenslander's dislike of those from the southern states, whom they referred to as 'Mexicans'. But I worked hard at establishing relationships, and gradually we achieved remarkable success. After six months or so, our sales justified importing containers directly into Brisbane from overseas suppliers. This also required us to acquire larger premises with an office, showroom, warehouse and service facilities, and to employ additional staff.

Having studied interior design during my time in the commercial furniture business, I was like a kid in a candy store having to set up a branch operation from the ground up. The showroom and offices were open plan, with an ultra-modern fit-out. The TV and audio service centre was something to behold, fitted out in white laminate workstations with mirrored back panels to reflect the rear working of equipment for the technicians. It was the absolute state of the art. We also had a warehouse large enough to accommodate deliveries of shipping containers.

Whilst everyone loved and admired our premises, the managing director was aghast at how much I had spent on it. Shortly after, the company chair made a flying visit to see me. I figured there was a fair chance my career with the company was about to come to a rapid end. But, to my surprise, having shown the chair through the building, he said, 'John, quality will be remembered long after price is forgotten', and he then took me out to dinner.

I have never forgotten this lesson and never compromise on quality – in everything. It also reminded me of something my mother often said to me – 'If the job's worth doing, it's worth doing well'.

We succeeded in making Queensland the most successful wholesale branch in the country, and the company used our state-of-the-art service facility for training purposes and as a design model for service agents nationally to emulate. As a result, the company's national service manager would regularly conduct his national technician training programs from our premises.

During my time in Brisbane, Rob Roberts had been appointed managing director of the entire AMI business and we got to work together. Rob was older than me and had far greater management experience, so apart from our friendship, he became my mentor and was responsible for shaping my management skills in areas like professionalism, attention to detail and managing people.

In December 1976, I was transferred back to Melbourne as the national marketing manager for the prestigious Blaupunkt television brand after AMI had moved into the TV business with the introduction of colour TV in Australia. Even though the product was more than twice the price of the market-leading brand, we managed a remarkable 10% market share in Australia.

My Blaupunkt strategy in Victoria was to form an 'exclusive club' with a select group of leading retail groups and home entertainment stores. We would conduct regular quarterly upmarket-themed dinners at our offices. They all had chairs with their names monogrammed on the back; the wait staff were all dressed in Lufthansa host uniforms, and we served gourmet food and wine. In the preamble to dinner, I would outline our marketing program and then provide them with my required product sales quotas for the year. If they were able to collectively commit to accept all the stock, which they always did, they retained exclusivity. At years end, they would all embark on a fully paid European tour, stopping off at Blaupunkt in Germany along the way. They loved it, and it was phenomenally successful for all concerned by providing exclusivity, profitability, personal enjoyment – oh, and as well as selling product.

Again, I had used the relationship and value-add strategy to achieve a successful outcome, which was a win-win for all concerned.

In around 1978, the decision was made to break up AMI into three joint venture companies between Brash and the relative overseas manufacturers. I was offered the chance to transfer to Brash's retail business as an audio/video product manager, which I accepted. This was an interesting transition, as the group retail managers saw me as coming from the 'dark side' of product wholesalers. I had to work hard to prove myself but was eventually taken into the retail fold.

I had already formed a relationship with Geoff Brash, but after joining the retail side of the business, I had much more to do with him, and he was always very generous with his time. He was an amazing man and had the extraordinary ability to communicate with every level of the organisation on an equal footing. He had the uncanny knack of remembering names and a snippet of personal information about everyone. I don't know how he did it, but it was inspirational. Geoff was also a strong believer in ethical behaviour and fair dealing, and I witnessed several examples of this during my time with the group. I have no doubt that many of my core beliefs were honed by the examples of Rob and Geoff.

After working for a time in product management, I was promoted to the position of regional manager, looking after several city and rural retail stores. On telling me this news, the managing director, who was a lifelong employee of the company and a devout retailer, informed me that, whilst the board had made the appointment, he had voted against it. Hardly encouraging words, I must say, but it certainly motivated me.

I decided to adopt a team approach to my group of stores, which was quite a change from the prior inter-store rivalry that existed. I met with my store managers at a central location each week to review performances and swap notes on strategies that had worked and those that had not. I introduced initiatives, such as stock sharing, in the hope that stores would be more willing to share their stock allocations with each other, and the group would then benefit overall. I also introduced a weekly newsletter with incentive programs for the store managers and the sales staff. There was initial pushback by the salespeople who did not want their performance judged publicly, but eventually they came around and enjoyed the experience and the rewards.

The outcome of my team's approach was that rather than trying to compete against each other, they added to each other's strengths and, as a group, were more successful. As a result of that, the entire group was more successful both in terms of sales and stock turnover efficiency.

Despite my promotion, I still spent time in the retail stores with my 'troops' so I could understand and share their challenges and look for ways to assist them in reaching their targets.

As our success as a group emerged, Geoff Brash took it upon himself to attend one of our weekly meetings, which was not only surprising but a huge compliment. My store managers got a great boost out of it, and I could see them walk a bit taller. I thought it was a notable example by Geoff of how great leaders should do the little things to get a disproportionate positive response.

This regime was extraordinarily successful, and our group usually outperformed other regional divisions of the retail chain through beating sales targets and managing stock efficiently, which benefitted all the store managers and did not do me any harm either. At my next review with the managing director, he admitted that he had been wrong and congratulated me on my achievements. Not only was I overjoyed and flattered by this, but I also thought it was a very magnanimous gesture on his part, and I admired him for it.

Each year, Brash's retail group (Brashs) held an annual dinner for all the company's store and divisional managers. Helen and I were honoured to be invited to sit with Geoff and Jenny Brash at their request. This was a huge honour and what I consider a high point in my professional career.

Rob Roberts had been appointed as managing director of one of the AMI joint venture businesses with Norlin Corporation in the United States (US). Norlin Music Australia marketed the Lowrey brand of home keyboards, which were extremely popular at that time.

I was approached by Denis Houlahan, the vice president of marketing for Norlin Music Corporation, who encouraged me to consider joining Norlin Music Australia in a marketing position. I expressed an interest, and Denis reported back to Rob Roberts. Rob had previously invited me to Lowrey marketing presentations, which were very theatrical and dynamic, so I figured there had to be some sort of prearranged subterfuge going on.

Now, I know nothing about music. I do not play a musical instrument, and I was not much interested in home keyboard music. But I was extremely interested in the theatrical and creative marketing, for which Lowrey was renowned, and a chance to work with a US-based company to broaden my marketing experience. Eventually, in 1980, I accepted the position of Australian marketing manager of Norlin Music Australia.

Geoff Brash arranged for farewell drinks for me in his office reception area, and I knew he was a little disappointed

I was leaving retail even though I was remaining in the group structure. I remember saying in my speech that I was not joining Norlin to leave Brashs but leaving Brashs to join Norlin for the experience I would gain.

My experience with Norlin Music was exciting, and we ran extraordinarily successful product releases with theatrical productions and all the razzamatazz you could imagine. I enjoyed my time at Norlin, but it was extremely demanding as I was continually travelling and away from my young family. In 1983, when a worldwide recession took place, US-produced product had great difficulty competing with their Japanese competitors, who had adopted a global price-cutting regime at that time. A prime example was when the iconic Harley-Davidson motorcycle brand was on the brink of bankruptcy due to the influx of cheaper and better engineered Japanese product in the US market. The market for home entertainment products was similarly tough and price sensitive.

Rob Roberts was at the Chicago home office when he called me and told me to jump on a plane and join them for an urgent strategy meeting. As it happened, Helen and I had already been talking about me looking for another job as the travel commitments with Norlin had become too much and I was rarely home. So, after the discussions in Chicago and despite reassurances from US management, it was clear to me that the short-term future looked grim. On the flight home with Rob, I suggested to him that it was time for me to go. He also had a marketing background, so there was not really room for us both in the current market conditions. I told him I would freelance, and he asked if I would subcontract my services to the company. We reached an agreement, and I called time on my corporate career.

During my time in the corporate management sector, I learnt about management structures' styles and behaviours – both good and bad. I found that the higher up the corporate management ladder I climbed, the more irrelevant it all became. More time was spent on political posturing than effective business management.

I recall an instance when I had a disagreement with the managing director over something that had become the gossip of the executive floor. I regularly had a morning coffee with the group's human resources manager and his assistant, but this particular morning they passed by my office and jokingly said they had to skip coffee with me that day as my 'star wasn't shining'. Funny but true.

These layered management structures were highly flawed, and I found it very frustrating. For example, when I was a divisional manager with Brashs, I made it my business to visit the retail stores under my watch on Friday nights, the busiest time of the week. The joint managing director, to whom I reported, called me into his office and told me that he regularly had drinks in his office on Friday at 4 pm and he expected me to be there. This was his way of gathering his troops around him as a show of force against his arch enemy, the other joint managing director, but hardly as important as enabling me to be out supporting my team on the front line.

Based on my experiences and beliefs in empowerment and flat management structures, I became very tired of the time wasted on keeping politically well placed at the expense of proactively managing the business or being home with my family. This was one of the dangers I was determined to avoid for my people in the future, and when I went into my own business, I discouraged people from working overtime and preached work-life balance. I repeatedly told my colleagues, if you cannot get your work done during normal work hours, you were either inefficient, disorganised or needed help. Of course, there will be times when long hours are unavoidable, but these must be exceptions to a general rule.

Chapter 3

On my own: a new beginning

1983

In 1983, I started out on my own, initially consulting with a family building business that specialised in building swimming pool enclosures. I helped them develop a business plan, took over their marketing and public relations, and became involved in selling their projects. We also started a joint business venture in swimming pool solar heating. As an aside, I also completed a diploma in landscape design during this time, which led to the development of another business. Norlin engaged me as a freelancer to head up their product release and training programs, as did their New Zealand counterpart. I had plenty to do, and it was financially rewarding, but nothing that represented a solid ongoing business venture that would grow beyond a one-man business.

In 1985, I began dabbling in the financial planning world whilst I continued with my consulting business. I quickly recognised this as a new opportunity to establish a professional advice practice that had the potential to build into a sustainable business in the future. The profession was in its infancy, but I could see the similarities with the accounting profession, which evolved over time into a recognised profession.

I remember being highly charged by the excitement of this business prospect and developing my business plan based on all the management concepts I had discovered during my experiences to date. Now I had the chance to develop them further in my own business. Also, I had trained as an accountant but never practiced in the profession. I saw this as an opportunity to develop a professional practice as well as a business opportunity.

Financial advice and securities dealing regulation fell under the National Companies and Securities Commission (NCSC). My first hurdle was to obtain a securities dealer representative licence, which had to be aligned to a licensed securities dealer, which in my case was Michael Wilson's company, Beyson Investment Services.

Beyson was owned by Wilson and two others in partnership with stockbroking firm McIntosh Hamson Hoar Govett. It was a significant player in the financial planning (FP) scene at that time.

I obtained my representative licence quite easily, which came as something of a surprise as I had no specific training or education in the field. But luckily, my accounting and business background was more than sufficient to satisfy the NCSC requirements. As I was soon to learn, there was no official qualification for securities advisers or financial planners in Australia at that time.

My training at Beyson was scant, to say the least, with an emphasis on product knowledge and sales. There was no importance given to the quality of advice or regulatory issues.

To clarify, I was self-employed by our own company but acting effectively as an agent of Beyson. My wife, Helen, was my secretary and the company's bookkeeper. We had to establish our own office and pay our own way until we were able to recruit new clients and generate revenue from fees charged to the client, of which we were paid a percentage, with Beyson retaining the balance.

Back in the 1980s, the financial services industry was controlled by large institutions like insurance companies and fund managers who designed and marketed investment products, with intermediary licensees like Beyson. The financial planner worked under what was called a 'proper authority', issued by the licensee, and were the self-employed marketing force that won the clients and provided capital input into investment products operated by the institutions. There was a toxic network of conflicts of interest and incentive payments that occurred throughout this structure. It was common practice for product manufacturers to offer and licensees to demand financial incentives for the support of their product on the licensees recommended investments list. This was clearly a conflict of interest in respect to recommending appropriate securities to clients.

I was never comfortable with or understanding of the almost pyramid-like business structure that existed in the industry. There were the financial institutions that developed the product, which was marketed via security dealer principals and their licensees. Then there were the advisers operating under authorities to the dealer principal licences. This all operated under a commission arrangement, where the institutions paid the dealers a commission and then the dealers paid the advisers an agreed share of the commission. In the 1980s, the rates of commissions paid on financial products were obscene. It was common for clients to pay upfront fees of around 5% simply to place money in a managed fund. Then there were outrageously high annual management fees charged by the fund managers, part of which were paid to the securities dealers as 'kickbacks' and volume incentives for supporting their products.

Apart from the inappropriateness of the commission system, there were too many 'snouts in the trough' and clients were paying outrageous costs for their money to be managed. Apart from the upfront commissions and charges, there were ongoing management fees based on a percentage of the client's funds invested, and advisers were paid a 'trailing commission', which was nothing more than a 'loyalty commission' to encourage advisors to retain clients' money in a manager's funds. Apart from the cost was the impact on advisers, who would be reluctant to advise their clients to make strategic changes to their portfolios just to retain their trail commissions. More conflict of interest.

Our company has always been fee-based and completely transparent with our clients. There are only two parties in our relationships, the client and their adviser, working in partnership to achieve the client's desired outcomes and protect their best interests. The investment piece is important, but it is simply a tool in the overall scheme of things and should not be the financial driver of the relationship.

I have no objection to salespeople being paid on commission for product sales or even volume bonuses, but when it comes to financial advice, it is inappropriate. Where advisers are remunerated by product manufacturers' commissions, there is automatically a conflict of interest. Whilst the strategic advice may be sound (and that is questionable), the selection of investment strategy will be biased by the terms of the commission arrangement and the adviser's relationship with parties other than solely with their client.

One example was when a financial planning colleague of mine invited me to join him on a field trip to a new viticulture venture in Northern Victoria. As we travelled on the bus, I read the investment prospectus, and the first thing I noted was that the adviser received a 10% upfront commission of any investment funds contributed. This also applied to leveraging through additional funds borrowed internally by the investor, so that someone investing say $20,000 and borrowing $20,000 would pay a commission of $4,000 upfront, plus management fees of 5%. This meant that the investor's own capital was already 20% in loss at the outset.

The justification for this investment was tax-driven, in that the investor got to claim a tax deduction for the capital invested. However, the closed-end period of the investment was seven years. Newly planted vines take six years to mature and produce, so there was virtually no chance of the investor making any capital profit. I immediately could see that the Australian Tax Office (ATO) would most likely question the legitimacy of the tax deductibility.

Sometime later, I ran into my colleague at a meeting, and he was quick to reach into his folder and proudly produce a commission cheque he had received for $100,000 for investing his clients' funds into this project. Later, I learnt that the scheme's tax deductibility was rejected by the ATO along with other similar schemes, creating massive losses for those who had invested. I rest my case.

The financial services industry had a history of dubious dealings and shonky schemes, but, finally, it went through a major restructure in recent years following the 2017 Hayne Royal Commission into Misconduct in the Banking, Superannuation and Financial Services Industry. This enquiry was to expose horrendous examples of bad conduct and consumer exploitation. Severe sanctions were imposed on major institutions including the major banks and other large institutions. It also highlighted deficiencies in the required educational standards for financial advisers. Due to the sanctions resulting from this inquiry and increased professional qualifications and practice standards for advisers, the major banks all sold their financial planning businesses and others who were not willing to meet the new standards disappeared from the profession.

Along with many of our professional colleagues, who had fought hard for over 20 years for action to be taken to clean up the industry and lift the regulated education standards, we applauded the Hayne findings and recommendations.

As we had instituted our own internal minimum education and practicing standards in the mid-1990s, we already exceeded the proposed standards, so it was business as usual for us. This relates to our core beliefs of honesty, integrity and fair dealing, professional excellence and people development, which we were never going to compromise on. I found it quite distressing being associated with the industry structure at the time, and there were a growing number of advisers that had similar beliefs to ours and saw the potential for the evolution of a true profession.

Besides feeling extremely uncomfortable about the structure of the industry at the time, I could never understand the viability or fairness of this industry structure. Financial advisers were effectively self-employed and were taking all the risks in meeting the costs of distribution, developing the markets and forming relationships with the clients. But due to the licensing system structure, clients were legally deemed to be effectively dealing with a licensee institution that they had never met and who controlled the revenue flow. Eventually this had to blow up – and it did.

Beyson operated a managed portfolio service, and all the business I developed with my clients flowed via this facility.

However, regardless of the relationship with Beyson, I went about developing my own business style and philosophy and saw Beyson as little more than an administrative necessity.

Chapter 4

Hewison Private Wealth: the establishment phase

1985–1987

We had our business plan; we had funding from liquidating our savings and had arranged additional funding through bank loans secured against our home. The pressure was now on to develop a market.

Getting the business off the ground was tough, as I started from ground zero and had to recruit prospective clients by knocking on doors. Fortunately, there was a crossover of income from my previous consulting business, from which I gradually withdrew whilst I built a new client base and a revenue stream from financial planning.

I was well out of my comfort zone having to cold call for clients after the security of a corporate senior management background. But in a way it was exhilarating, and as I gradually found success, my motivation grew.

I knew that trying to recruit individual clients directly would be an impossible task and would result in a transactionally-based business, that is, a business that relied on finding individual prospective clients on a daily basis. I needed to establish a referral network with a pool of prospective clients I could access. I concentrated primarily on accounting firms with an existing client base who would be requiring financial planning advice.

Unfortunately, accountants saw financial planners as the new kids on the block who posed a competitive threat, and they generally had a low opinion of them. This was partly because the early financial planners came from the life insurance industry and were seen as commission salespersons. Sadly, this was justified, and in the 1980s it was like the Wild West, and I found it hard to cope with the poor image of financial planners. I remember attending a friend's housewarming party and talking to a group of men who I hadn't previously met. When they asked me what I did for a living, I proudly announced that I was a financial planner. A member of the group immediately retorted, 'You mean a glorified insurance salesman'. I was aghast, insulted and angry at this comment and walked away in disgust. As I stewed in a corner considering confronting this fellow, I had to admit to myself that his comment was probably reflective of the image financial planners had at that time, and it was probably justified. I was convinced that financial planning was a distinct and honourable profession and that, eventually, it would evolve and be recognised as such.

I set about writing to 160 accounting firms in the CBD of Melbourne and the inner southern suburbs. Then I got on the telephone and systematically called them. Most were not interested or asked me to call back later, so I diarised and then called them back. Gradually, some started to agree to see me, and the others I rescheduled and called back until they agreed to a meeting or told me to go away.

With the advantage of my accounting training and business background, I could quickly establish a connection, communicate with accountants on their level, and they did not see me as a threat. Whilst it took considerable time and effort to establish relationships, I gained the trust of accounting firms who were prepared to refer their clients to me.

In the early days, we offered to split fees for referrals, but I quickly learnt that (a) highly professional accounting firms did not want financial incentives, simply good service, and (b) the stronger relationships were those built on trust rather than financial incentive. Eventually, all our referral relationships were non-financial, and as we grew, we were able to cross-refer clients, so there was a mutual benefit in the relationship, many of which have endured for over 30 years.

Our business is simple. It is about recruiting new clients through developing a caring personal relationship and providing sound professional advice and ongoing management of their personal affairs.

Most financial planners did not understand the purity and simplicity of this business. They become ensconced in the world of investment markets and the belief that the skill and expertise their clients seek is the investment piece. Consequently, financial advisers became seen as commission-based product floggers or held accountable for beating market returns.

But in my world, nothing could be further than the truth. Yes, clients want their financial adviser to make sound investments for them, but it is the broader outcome that is important. It is the achievement of their hopes and dreams and the things they are most passionate about that matter the most to them. And it is about the trusting relationship they have with their adviser.

Financial advisers who focus on the investment piece effectively develop a transactional business. That is, they concentrate on creating an investment portfolio that may be based on some sort of risk profiling tool and forget about developing an ongoing relationship with the client. So effectively, these advisers must restart their business every day looking for the next transaction. And this is true of any business. It is important to try and create ongoing relationships and, preferably, a continuous revenue stream, thus creating intrinsic value.

My view of financial planning is that it is an intimate, lifelong relationship. In fact, it should be a multi-generational business, as we often manage multiple generations in the one family and philosophically believe in multi-generational wealth transfer, which I will discuss in greater detail later. We charge clients a professional fee for developing an initial bespoke and comprehensive financial strategy plan, which is effectively a blueprint for the future, taking all their circumstances, objectives, goals and dreams into account. Once appointed, we charge an ongoing monthly fee for managing their affairs, regularly reviewing the plan, and updating the plan according to inevitable changes in their circumstances. This becomes a very close relationship and has resulted in many former clients becoming long-lasting friends.

From a business perspective, this model enabled us to develop internal systems and infrastructure to manage our clients' affairs efficiently and deliver high-level, quality service at a competitive price. Financially, it progressively developed into a recurrent annual revenue stream accounting for more than 90% of the company's income. This made the business financially secure but also translated into an incredibly attractive intrinsic market value. From a service delivery aspect, it enabled us to provide our clients with the proactive continuous management of their affairs both efficiently and economically. It also achieved another one of our core beliefs and key elements of our business plan.

In the words of President Theodore Roosevelt, 'People don't care how much you know until they know how much you care'. Never a truer word has been spoken.

Those in any business or profession are salespeople. All through my marketing and sales background, I managed to achieve an extremely high success rate, and I put that down to my belief that selling was not about selling a product or a service but about problem-solving or satisfying a need. Sales is the skill of discovering what people desire and providing a solution to that desire. But discovering that desire can only be done through the development of a trusting relationship with the client.

Whilst over the years, we have developed a high-quality service offering to our high-net-wealth financial planning clients, our main emphasis is about developing relationships so that clients become comfortable sharing their most sensitive personal aspirations. This may sound simplistic, but when it comes to wealth aspirations, most people have deep-seated personal ambitions that they may not be comfortable sharing easily. I have often encountered situations where life partners have not even shared their financial hopes and dreams with each other, and this has led to some very emotional conversations. But in the final analysis, this is manifestly more important than what securities we might choose to invest in. It is a bit like planning a long journey – you need to develop a road map aimed at achieving the desired destination before you choose how to get there.

The problem-solving or achieving 'goals and dreams' proposition applies to any business and profession. Focusing on what is truly important to the client is essential to success in any field.

I could recount hundreds of examples of the importance of client relationships, but I distinctly recall two instances that vividly illustrate this point at the outset.

The first instance was a married couple who came to an initial meeting with me. He was a barrister, and she was a stay-at-home mum at the time. We had an hour-long discussion about

Pooled mortgage income funds were frozen for months so that clients could not get access to their money. It was ugly and exposed the weaknesses of managed fund structures and their management.

One vivid memory I have of this time is when, just before the market crash, a retired estate agent came to see me having been referred by his accountant. He had sold his business and had a considerable sum of money to invest. He had read about an extremely high-risk managed fund that had been boasting astonishing returns, and he wanted to invest in it. I tried to counsel him against this high-risk strategy, but, in the end, he insisted on investing. I refused to transact it for him despite the large amount of commission I would have been entitled to receive. It would have been professionally and morally wrong, and I did not want to be responsible if the worst happened. Unfortunately, he went to another adviser who did invest in the fund for him, and sadly, when the market crashed, the fund collapsed, and he lost everything. His accountant later told me that he had to return to work.

Another problem with managed structures is that an individual investor, who might take the sensible approach and decide to hold their investment in times of market volatility, is being disadvantaged by other investors in the fund who are selling out at the wrong time, leaving the patient, cool-headed investor with a compromised, reduced-value portfolio. A further consequence is that the sale of shares within the portfolio may have crystallised capital gains accumulated over time, which could cause the investor a capital gains tax obligation, adding insult to injury.

When markets fall due to an external phenomenon, such as a credit crisis or an extraordinary event like the 9/11 terrorist attacks in the US, it does not necessarily mean that the intrinsic values of individual company shares fall, nor does it mean that their profitability is adversely affected. Therefore, it is not the time to sell, and moreover, it presents valuable opportunities to buy undervalued assets with attractive dividend income streams. It never fails to amaze me when people act in such an illogical manner, but it always happens. To quote Warren Buffet, 'We simply attempt to be fearful when others are greedy and greedy only when others are fearful'.

The 1987 stock market crash occurred at the height of a 5-year bull market, which was primarily triggered by programmed computerised selling in the US. Major investment institutions use computer programming as risk management mechanisms to react to various changes in market conditions. In this case, a set of market-based criteria occurred, causing mass computer selling to be automatically triggered. Once this happened, prices fell, fear set in and panic selling occurred.

We worked proactively and tirelessly, communicating with our clients and working to recover their financial position. But I was frustrated with the lack of flexibility in their portfolio structures and the inability for us to take advantage of obvious opportunities to invest directly in quality, share-market listed investments that were ridiculously undervalued. It was so infuriating when we could see the value in investing but were unable to access client funds to take advantage.

I should also point out that Beyson had a discretionary authority to invest clients' money without first seeking individual approval. This meant that they were buying bulk quantities of ASX shares in Melbourne on Monday 19 October 1987. So, before they had even been allocated to individual clients' accounts, they had fallen in value by around 40% the next day. You can imagine how clients felt finding out that they had lost money before they even owned the investments. Consequently, we do not seek or believe in discretionary investment authority. We insist on recommending investments to clients and requiring their agreement before we act and have subsequently designed systems that enable us to send advice to our clients electronically for immediate approval and timely implementation.

As an example of the market madness, a company called Cumberland Credit had floated on the ASX just before the 1987 crash. It was a 'cashbox' company that simply raised funds to invest in a portfolio of shares listed on the stock market. At the time of the market crash, Cumberland had not invested and held nothing but cash deposits with a cash asset backing of $1.10 per share. Its share price fell to 60 cents, which equates to buying $1.10 cash for a market price of 60 cents. Likewise, blue-chip shares, like the four major banks, fell around 40%, resulting in their gross dividends equating to a return of around 12% per annum, not to mention the huge capital upside. This was a no-brainer, but we could not take full advantage of it. I resolved that something had to change.

We decided that we had to find a way to abandon managed investment structures and buy direct investments for our clients, so they retained absolute control over their own destinies and had the flexibility to act, when necessary, where opportunities existed.

This was to be the core of our investment and management philosophy for the future, which I will expand on further.

In the meantime, my personal assistant (PA), Janine, who had stated to me prior to her appointment that 'I am a PA - I don't do figures', had become highly proficient at correcting

Beyson's client reports and 'doing figures'. We both had a keen interest in information technology (IT), which was very much in its infancy in those days, and we were inspired to seek an alternative route to deliver better outcomes for our clients.

My financial planning colleagues referred to me as the 'fund manager' because we invested clients in direct shares and direct interest-bearing securities. But the reality is that adequate spread can be achieved with minimal cost by investing directly, where the client controls the ownership of their investment and the resultant cash flow. Simplistic, yes, but highly effective. But just as importantly, we developed close client relationships and we managed our clients' affairs in-house, so we had the ability and the flexibility to act in their best interests and achieve positive results.

Another lesson I learnt was the propensity for financial advisers to use 'risk profiling' as the dictator of portfolio asset allocation, which is the balance between different investment sectors such as fixed interest, property, domestic and international shares. This entailed the use of a simplistic questionnaire on attitudes towards risk, which generated a point score that determined the client's risk profile. That, in turn, determined the client's asset allocation and, in most cases, a computer-generated portfolio of investments.

There are issues with this system, however, which was really a compliance tool designed to protect the licensee. But my key issues are firstly, everyone is risk averse, it is only a question of the level of sensitivity. Next is the understanding of the difference between investment volatility and the risk of loss. Volatility is when market prices fluctuate due to external influences rather than any change to the intrinsic value of an investment as distinct from the actual loss of value. One of my major, long-term clients, who was a sophisticated business owner, used to taking business risk once said to me, 'John, it has taken me many years to build my wealth, so don't you f------g lose it.' Does this mean that I should not expose him to investment assets that might experience short-term market volatility? Not at all.

The risk profiling approach has been enshrined in the regulations governing financial planning licensing requirements, which in my view is inappropriate in isolation. But there are also requirements to 'know your client' and provide advice that is appropriate to their circumstances.

My view was that I had a responsibility to design a strategic plan and an investment portfolio that were specifically aimed at achieving a client's stated outcomes in the most risk effective way. It was then my responsibility to explain the issues of volatility, security of investment income, and the nature of specific investments, and gaining the client's confidence. Thereafter, it was a matter of managing the portfolio strategy with a strict protocol of review and rebalancing back to the original asset allocation strategy.

We are great believers in the concept of multi-generational wealth transfer. This relates to the concept of designing long-term strategies for our clients that will build their capital to a point where it has sufficient income generation to provide for their long-term living needs and sufficient capital to provide for large expenditure items according to their express wishes.

Most clients have a desire to assist their families in ways such as assisting with a residential purchase or paying private school fees for grandchildren. In addition, they have a desire to leave a legacy to their descendants. We refer to this as multi-generational wealth transfer.

Designing portfolio strategies for multi-generational purposes changes the dynamic entirely and renders the industry 'risk profiling' model completely inappropriate.

Interestingly, in around 1995, I had a visit at my office with the then deputy commissioner for the Australian Securities Commission (ASC), which was the regulatory authority of the day. I knew him quite well through my industry experience, and he just wanted to have a chat. He expressed the view that it was just a matter of time until a financial planner would face a complaint from a client whose funds had deteriorated through an ultra-conservative investment strategy based on a risk profile rather than one reflecting the client's specific needs for capital protection.

The close relationship we built with our clients meant that over time they became empowered to understand short-term market volatility and the power of disciplined portfolio rebalance. They recognised that market volatility was a chance to buy quality assets at a cheap price, thus providing capital growth opportunity and achieving attractive income returns.

Whilst this is all specifically related to investment management, it relates to the difference between commoditisation of professional advice and automated portfolio construction versus relationship-driven advice and bespoke portfolio construction, specifically aimed at achieving specific outcomes for the client. In other words, providing specific outcomes for specific client needs requires bespoke portfolios designed for individual clients to achieve specific outcomes.

I remember once attending a conference session presented by three fund managers specialising in shares, bonds and property. They were each asked to address specific sets of client circumstances and asked to outline their strategic advice. At the same time, the audience, consisting of financial advisers, was asked to prepare their strategic solutions. The outcome was that the fundies argued their own investment theories whilst the advisers argued about portfolio models. Our response was to design portfolios that specifically addressed the stated outcomes in the case studies, like income requirements, longer-term estate requirements and other issues raised in the client case studies. We were able to specifically address the client issues, whilst the other outcomes were purely based on theoretical assumptions.

Chapter 6

Who owns the client?

1988–1989

In the wake of the 1987 share market crash, Beyson's partners, stockbroker McIntosh Securities, had decided they wanted to dispose of the company due to the outfall from the market crash. Upon learning of this, the key financial advisers, including me, decided to look for alternative licensee opportunities.

Beyson was sold to ASX-listed company Stenhouse Securities Ltd and shortly after, Michael Wilson, who was one of Beyson's owners, was terminated. He approached me to see if he could rent space from us, knowing that we had a vacant office following Rob Robert's departure. I agreed.

Wilson had retained his licence authority with Stenhouse and moved into our offices, bringing a small number of his existing clients with him. My arrangement with Wilson was simply a sublet, and we operated completely independent of one another. He was off looking for new schemes to make money, and I continued looking after my clients as usual. But as the heat intensified around the move to Stenhouse, we were both anxious to part company with them to pursue an alternative securities dealer.

I notified Stenhouse of my intention to leave and offered to send a joint communique with them to the client base advising of my departure.

I had a contract with Stenhouse that contained a restraint in the event of me leaving but required them to pay me a considerable amount of money for my client base. History had shown that the restraint was not worth the paper it was written on, as the client could choose to leave and follow the adviser of their own volition. I was constrained from approaching the client, but, of course, having such a close relationship, the client was always going to enquire where I was going. Hence, I thought my offer to send the joint communiqué was fair and let the clients choose, bearing in mind that I would not be paid for clients who chose to follow me.

Stenhouse not only refused my offer but told me that they were going to enforce the restraint and not pay me anything for the clients. I was then left with no option but to sue Stenhouse for breach of contract and a claim for the payment required under the terms of my contract. They in turn countersued, claiming I had breached my restraint. They were a public company with large financial resources, and clearly their tactic was to stretch this out until I ran out of money.

Having discussed this matter with my existing lawyer, I concluded that this matter was beyond him, and I needed to appoint legal muscle to assume this fight. I appointed leading law firm Arnold Bloch Leibler to represent me and quickly realised that, whilst this was a good decision, it was going to be expensive, and Helen and I had to borrow significantly to cover operating costs and legal costs.

I was advised that we had a compelling case and a particularly good chance of success if I was careful not to break my restraint requirements.

I subsequently sent a carefully worded letter to clients (based on my barrister's advice), notifying them that I had left

Stenhouse. As expected, the phone melted down with clients wanting to know what I was doing, and as soon as they asked that question, I was at liberty to tell them. If they then asked if they could come with me, I was entitled to say yes and thereafter talk freely.

As a result of all this, a substantial portion of our clients followed me over time, but we lost clients from one accounting firm who decided to go into the financial planning business themselves.

The matter stretched out for months due to Stenhouse's procrastination at every turn, and then there was the delay in the Supreme Court calendar.

The hearing date arrived, and my lawyer and barrister were both confident. But facing court is a different thing and was extremely stressful and demoralising. I could not believe the testimony given by former senior management colleagues from Beyson, who were now with the Stenhouse management team. I do not accuse them of deliberately lying but certainly their recollections were quite different from the facts as I knew them. They even tried to deny that the compensation clause in my agreement was legitimate and that I had somehow inserted it into my agreement. Then the opposing barrister saw fit to try and discredit me and accuse me of all sorts of wrongdoing and breaching my contract restraint. It was a harrowing day, to say the least, and my confidence began to slip.

Wilson was called as a witness on my behalf, given his position with Stenhouse at the time of the contract signing. He came over as something of a used car salesperson, and I would have been better off without him.

After a full day of cross-examination by both sides, the judge stopped proceedings following the opposing barrister's summation of their case. I sat there petrified at the outcomes. The judge told my barrister he did not need to hear from him and set about admonishing the defendant's legal team for the unreasonableness of their position and the claims against me. He found in my favour and awarded the full amount of the contract sum and applied interest on the payment for the period since I left. He also awarded costs against the other side.

I sat there stunned and completely washed out. I was numb and mentally exhausted. My lawyer and barrister turned around in delight and congratulated me. Then I listened to them congratulating each other about the clever tactics they had used and talked a bit like a prize fighter after winning a championship fight. 'How about when I hit them with that and then defended with that ...'. It was like a game to them. And then they walked out of the court in smiling conversation with the opposition barrister, who had given me such a rough time. An extraordinary experience I would not want to repeat!

What a relief I foolishly felt, as more was yet to come.

Stenhouse was instructed to pay me 50% of my contract amount up front plus interest and pay my legal costs. They were to pay the balance in 12 months time. Stenhouse then set about ignoring my lawyers repeated demands for payment, and we finally had to summon a court sheriff to deal with the matter – at a cost of course. We received the initial payment, but that did not even cover our legal costs.

Then came the process of 'costing' legal fees. This is a process conducted by an officer of the court to estimate a reasonable cost to run the case in question. The actual cost was around $60,000. The court estimate was $14,000. So much for awarding costs!

After 12 months, I contacted my lawyer to see how we went about claiming the second payment of fees owing to me as awarded by the court. Not surprisingly, Stenhouse refused to pay. When I asked my lawyer what action we could take, he told me we would have to go back to court. I said thanks but no thanks and moved on.

So, in conclusion of this challenge, I might have had the satisfaction of winning the argument, but it wasted countless hours in time, I endured considerable stress, and we were left with a hefty loan for the balance of the legal fees.

Another lesson learnt – whatever you do, stay out of court!

Postscript

This was an important legal test case for the financial services profession in that the licensee/agent structure was seriously flawed. The institutional licensees believed they had ownership of the client base, and in the event of the proper authority holder or agent leaving, they had no right of ownership. But in fact, the licensee had no direct relationship with the client at all. In fact, in most cases, the client didn't understand the licensee to representative structure and only ever had contact with their adviser. Consequently, the only relationship that existed was that between the adviser and the client, everything else was simply irrelevant to the client.

The reality is that no-one 'owns' the client; it is the client alone who will decide with whom they wish to deal. And they will inevitably choose the person with whom they have a relationship, that being their adviser.

Years later, I had a meeting with the chairman and another director of a listed conglomerate who was putting together a company acquiring accounting and financial planning firms with a view to listing on the ASX. I knew the chairman, who had met with me previously, and although I hadn't met his fellow director, he was familiar to me. It turned out that he had been a director of Stenhouse Securities when I sued them, and he was quite amused when I recognised him. He told me that they had deliberately drawn out the legal process and had expected me to run out of money and go away. I gained some further satisfaction out of rejecting their proposal and showing them the door.

Chapter 7

My foray into partnership

During 1988, Wilson and I collaborated on finding a new licensee. During this negotiation, Wilson suggested that we join forces to broker a better deal as a joint entity. I eventually agreed, based on Wilson's experience at Beyson but against the advice of Helen and Janine, both of whom had little regard for Wilson.

We changed our licensee arrangements to FPI Pty Ltd, which was another licensed securities dealer and a division of the Norwich Insurance Group. FPI were pleasant to deal with, offered good support and had an internal portfolio management system we could readily adapt to meet our needs. Their systems did not entirely provide what we wanted to achieve, but they allowed us to collaborate with their programmers to develop our own internal IT portfolio management system. This worked well but was still manual and supported by spreadsheets, which Janine and I had developed.

Whilst Wilson and I had formed a joint venture company in late 1988, we continued to work independently of each other with respect to our client management and did not have contact with each other's clients. I continued developing my financial planning clients and referral networks whilst Wilson looking after his small client base and continued to develop a variety of money-making schemes.

Wilson was not a particularly close friend of mine, but I quickly came to learn that he was almost illiterate – shocking grammar and poor mathematics. He tended to be quite aggressive at times, and I often had to repair damage he caused in discussions with business colleagues and staff. This was particularly so of our FPI licensing partners, with whom he thought he could be overly aggressive and demanding due to his Beyson experience.

I became tired of Wilson's lack of presence in the business as he was often away and produced little new business for the company. This, added to his behaviour, prompted me to confront him.

Wilson brought questionable 'business opportunities' to the table, but they were all akin to get-rich-quick schemes with little relevance to our core business. I recall one such proposition where Wilson had negotiated a deal with a large insurance company to give us a $1 million 'development loan'. In return, we would provide them with access to our client base for marketing their insurance products. This was frequent practice at that time of intense competition between insurance companies. I sat there listening to this nonsense in the knowledge that most of the client base was mine, and I had no intention of selling access to anyone, let alone an insurance company.

As soon as they were gone, I made it quite clear to Wilson that I was not interested, and it was not going to happen. He was furious, and I saw another side of his aggressive personality.

In 1989, Wilson took on the management of a high-profile AFL (Australian Football League) footballer who was a controversial figure with a propensity for getting into trouble and defying authority. Wilson became obsessed with this role, which became a time-consuming distraction and occupied most of his time without much reward. The footballer was always newsworthy and often involved in controversy of one sort or another. Wilson had become infatuated with the notoriety as I grew even more impatient with Wilson's lack of contribution to the business.

During 1990, I was sitting in Wilson's office when he brought up the subject of fixed interest investing and how he thought he might start using bank term deposits for his clients. I remember this being quite an odd thing for him to say, and although it did not particularly worry me at the time, it certainly stuck in my mind.

Early in 1991, Wilson rang me at home one night to advise me that he had been diagnosed with bowel cancer and would require immediate surgery. I was shocked, and despite our troubled relationship, I had sympathy for him and undertook to support him fully through this dreadful time. He subsequently had the surgery and then underwent his first course of treatment lasting several weeks.

During the months following, I worked seven days a week, keeping the business afloat and visiting Wilson most nights. He eventually finished his treatment and was given a clean bill of health. I obviously expected him to make a return to the business since I had been supporting him financially and personally and had kept the business going. It had been a huge strain on me and my family, but I had no regrets.

To my surprise, Wilson hardly showed his face in the office and seemed to be preoccupied doing other things. He bought himself a Mercedes Benz, new clothes, a boat and went on extended holidays. I could not believe it! I assumed he was more concerned with living the good life in the wake of his cancer scare, but given the sacrifices that I and my family had made to support him in his battle, I resented his lack of resolve to make a reasonable contribution to the business once he had recovered.

At this point, I should point out that I had always assumed that Wilson had money, as I knew he had sold his interest in Beyson for around $1 million in 1988. So, I was not particularly suspicious of his spending at the time.

When he embarked on yet another holiday on a Whitsunday Island, I lost patience. He rang to check in, and I told him the party was over and I wanted to end the relationship. He hightailed it home on the next plane, and we lunched the next day. He was apologetic, remorseful and promised to mend his ways. I reluctantly agreed to give him one more chance. Then shortly after, in mid-1991, Wilson told me that the cancer had returned and was now in his liver. He said that his specialist had recommended that he travel to the US for laser surgery that was not available in Australia at that time. He subsequently left with his family in August 1991 to have the required surgery.

Whilst Wilson was away, I was working in my office one Wednesday in late August when Janine came in with a curious look on her face. She told me a client had just called and asked about a withdrawal of $30,000 from her account. Janine replied that it was the Commonwealth Bank (CBA) term deposit that Wilson had discussed with her. The client said she knew nothing about it. I immediately recalled the conversation I had with Wilson months earlier, where he strangely commented about putting clients' money into term deposits. My blood ran cold.

I asked Janine to give me the date of the transaction. She came back and told me with a look of dread on her face as I went to the safe where Wilson kept his bank books. I pulled out his CBA deposit book and turned to the page dated the same as the client transaction. There was a deposit of $30,000, which matched the client's cheque. My heart sank, and at that moment, I saw my career flash before my eyes and assumed it was over. Janine was screaming, 'What is it?' I told her Wilson had stolen the client's money.

I asked Janine to what extent similar transactions had been made, and she said there were a considerable number. I asked her to go through all Wilson's clients' accounts and list all similar transactions or anything that looked suspicious or unusual. As she compiled the list, I kept checking, and, sure enough, there were matching deposits in Wilson's personal bank accounts.

The next day I was scheduled to drive to Horsham, a major rural town in Victoria about a 4-hour drive from my home. I had an accountant colleague there, with whom we had a referral relationship, and I had made appointments to see several of our mutual clients during the day. I arose at 4 am, skipped breakfast as I could not eat, and drove in a trance with my head spinning with the thoughts and ramifications of the previous day.

Having managed to get through the day's meetings, punctuated by updates from Janine, I headed for home exhausted. As I passed through Ballarat, about halfway home, I nodded off to awake with a start just before I drove into the freeway barrier fence. I wrenched the steering wheel, narrowly avoiding disaster. I was visibly shaking but managed to navigate my way home without further incident. I was living a nightmare and had no idea how it was going to play out.

By Friday night, we had discovered $250,000 of fraudulent transactions with still more checking to be done. I knew Wilson was going to telephone me from the US on Sunday, so I decided to defer any decisions until after then.

On the evening of Sunday 25 August, my 44th birthday, Wilson called from his hospital room in the US. He started chatting in good humour until I stopped him and told him I knew about the withdrawals from his client's accounts. He paused and said, 'Oh, you mean the loans?' I replied that 'Loans are when people know about them, and that is not the case.' I told him that we had traced the transactions and knew that what he purported to be for term deposits amounted to $250,000.

There was stony silence, and then he confessed. He asked me what I was going to do, and I told him that I didn't know. In my confusion, I stupidly said that I might have to take a loan on my house to repay the money. He said he had to go, then asked me not to tell any of his family as he wanted to tell them himself. Again, stupidly, I gave him my word.

Chapter 8

Dealing with the fraud

By Monday night, following my confrontation with Wilson, Janine informed me that we had now discovered $1 million of fraudulent transactions. Clearly, with Wilson's confession and the extent of his fraudulent activities, I had no option but to notify our licensee and report the matter to the police. Apart from my licensing responsibility, there was no way I could find that sort of money to buy our way out of trouble, so I needed to inform our professional indemnity (PI) insurer to protect the clients' interests and ensure we could gain access to our PI insurance. PI insurance provides protection to the business against damages and against client claims for losses suffered due to malpractice or deception by its employees. It also provides client compensation for any losses sustained as a result. At this point, I had no concern about Wilson and wanted him brought to justice.

I called Tony, the CEO of FPI, and told him the shocking news. Somehow, he did not seem surprised given his turbulent experiences with Wilson. He told me that he would do everything he could to support us in sorting this out. He would first need to inform the regulator, the Australian Securities Commission (ASC) (now the Australian Securities and Investments Commission – ASIC) and discover what action they would want to take. Then he would get back to me to formulate a plan of action.

I called our PI insurer and spoke to a claims manager who was extremely helpful. He made it clear that, in the circumstances, it was their primary responsibility to protect me and the company as the insured, but he also made it clear that they would pursue Wilson. He told me I was not to give any guarantees to the clients that their money would be repaid until an investigation was completed. I asked him to give me a set of words I could use that would give the clients some level of comfort, which he did. He told me that he would notify their lawyers, Minter Ellison, to conduct an audit of our business and determine the facts of the fraud.

The next day I went to police headquarters, which was also located in St Kilda Road, just a short walk from our office. I was directed to the fraud squad and met with a very obliging and helpful detective sergeant. I explained the situation, and he said that he would arrange for detectives to call at our office the next day.

Then I called my good friends at Arnold Bloch Leibler to advise them what had happened and obtain preliminary legal guidance, which they did after I paid their retainer. This was going to be another expensive exercise.

The FPI CEO called back after a couple of days and advised that the ASC had suspended Wilson's licence but had agreed to allow my licence to remain intact, pending an investigation. He further advised that FPI's compliance officer would be paying me a visit, and they would also undertake an audit investigation as part of their compliance requirements.

ASC auditors landed on our doorstep to carry out an audit of our files. Our PI insurers advised that their lawyers, Minter Ellison, would be carrying out an audit of our files to ensure we were compliant and were conducting the investigation thoroughly. In addition to their compliance audit, FPI engaged an auditor to carry out an independent investigation of our files and our handling of the overall situation.

We were inundated with investigators and auditors, which was a harrowing experience, particularly for Janine, who had always had the view that auditors were out to prove she was a criminal. But, nevertheless, we successfully got through all this with a big tick from all.

Following the ASC investigation, which took all of two days, the investigators congratulated us on our systems and how we were handling the matter. FPI contacted me again, advising that the ASC were satisfied that we had the matter under control, and they were happy for us to manage it. They said that my licence was safe, but I had to shut down the operations of the company and transfer the clients from the company entity to me personally as a sole trader. We had to change the locks on the office doors and ensure that Wilson would not gain access or contact clients.

Whilst this was a mammoth administration job, it went smoothly, except for the financial ramifications of transferring clients to me as a sole trader. This meant that all revenue became what is termed 'personal exertion' and thus fully income taxable. I could not offset running costs until I filed my tax return, so what was left of our usable revenue was effectively halved.

We struggled to remain financially viable, and we had no more scope to borrow. Our main income was paid quarterly, and we often ran out of money in the interim. The most humbling of experiences to come out of this disaster was how all our suppliers, accountant colleagues, industry contacts and clients supported us unconditionally. Our stockbroker friends at D&D Tolhurst Ltd often lent us money to see us through, which we paid back at quarter end. Our printer printed all our new stationery and told us to pay when we could. It brought tears to my eyes.

I clearly remember calling a professional colleague and friend of mine, and his wife answered the telephone. She knew of my dilemma and sympathised, saying, 'The hotter the fire, the stronger the steel.' I kept that in mind when things got bad and have never forgotten it.

As I noted in our core beliefs, honesty, fair trading and treating people with respect were important to me. We always paid our bills on time or early, had fabulous personal relationships with everyone we dealt with and built our business on long-term relationships. No doubt, this trust and respect was now coming back to us in spades. It was very humbling.

The fraud squad detectives were terrific, and as we took them through all our discovery, they could not wipe the smile off their faces. They explained that they had never been presented with such a complete set of evidence or an audit trail of fraudulent transactions and a source to obtain a paper trail of proof.

Our portfolio management systems were designed around the cash account. That is, we would balance everything back to the client's portfolio bank account daily. We had a policy that we would not account for investments that we did not physically hold on the client's behalf. Therefore, if funds were withdrawn for the purchase of an asset that we did not hold, we would treat it as a withdrawal with appropriate notation. This was designed to be a self-auditing mechanism that we could monitor daily, down to the cent, ensuring that clients could obtain accurate information. But this also enabled us to isolate all transactions that were purported to be for external investments or client requests and easily determine if they were fraudulent transactions.

Whilst all this was going on, Janine and I had to undertake the arduous task of visiting all the clients affected and explaining to them what had happened. These people were elderly and had been completely trusting of Wilson. To tell them that he had been stealing their life savings was heartbreaking for all concerned, including us. It was made even more difficult as, although Janine had dealt with them on the telephone, I had no relationship with them at all. We relayed our PI insurer's set of words, which gave them comfort, and assured them that we would not rest until we achieved a positive outcome for them.

One day during this time, I received a telephone call from one of Wilson's clients who had not been a victim. They insisted that I visit them at their home in Mount Eliza, an outer Melbourne suburb. I did not know these people, and I was suspicious, but I had to agree. Janine and I visited their house, which was situated on heavily treed acreage. We went inside and proceeded to tell them what had happened and assured them they had not been a victim of these crimes. As we left, I noticed the back of Wilson's car parked behind a shed.

The clients called us a couple of weeks later and aggressively requested that all their files and investments be sent to their address, which we duly arranged. Ironically, some months later, the wife rang me to advise that Wilson has stolen their money and asked if we would take them back and help them seek compensation. I politely declined.

During Wilson's absences from the business, I had been overseeing the management of his football client. After auditing his accounts, we concluded that he had suffered no loss from Wilson's activities, but nevertheless, I had to meet with him and his father to advise them of the situation. Shortly thereafter, we received a call from a lawyer based in Dandenong, an outer suburb of Melbourne, advising us that he had been appointed to take over the player's management. He requested that we pack up all the client's files and send them to his office immediately, which we did.

Weeks later, the player's lawyer called again and requested a 'negotiation' meeting, to which I again advised that his client had suffered no loss. He did not agree and insisted upon the meeting. I called the PI insurance lawyer, who told me one of his lawyer colleagues would accompany me to the meeting.

We met with the lawyer at his Dandenong office, which was something of a dumping ground for horse racing memorabilia and paperwork, including the client's stack of unopened file boxes we had sent to him.

I explained again that there was no evidence of loss to his client at all. He simply said that if his client did not get money, he would be very unhappy. He then told us he would take our company to court, obtain a judgement and set about destroying my personal reputation. He then pointed to me directly and said that his client had very nasty friends who carried guns and would be around to visit me at my house. My lawyer was aghast at this threat and said, 'You can't say that!', to which came the reply, 'I can say what I like. This meeting is 'in camera' (legal jargon meaning 'in confidence'), to which my lawyer responded, 'We didn't agree to that.' He simply said, 'I don't care'.

We left the meeting in a state of shock and just stood outside, looking incredulously at each other. The PI lawyer gathered himself together and told me that their priority would be to keep me and the company out of court and to protect my reputation. He said he would discuss everything with his colleagues and get back to me.

Later that day, the PI lawyer called and said that they had negotiated a sum of $27,000 to pay off the player's lawyer. The insurer had agreed to pay half if we would pay half too, to which

I reluctantly but readily agreed. This was pure extortion, but I was grateful for the pragmatic view taken by the insurer to protect our interests.

I had been given a death threat, and I do not mind admitting I was scared, for both myself and my family. For weeks, I kept checking outside the house to see if anyone was there.

I had not heard anything from Wilson for weeks. I did not even know if he was back in Australia. Then I had a call from his wife, with whom I had a good relationship. She asked me what was going on, and I queried if he had told her. She said that he had given her some story that I had done the wrong thing by him. I assured her that this was not the case, that it was serious, and she needed to force him to tell her what he had done. So much for giving assurances to Wilson, but I was not able to tell her the facts in case I got accused of defamation, as he had not been found guilty in a court of law.

The next thing I know, I get a call from my lawyer advising me that he had been approached by a lawyer acting for Wilson. They were suing me for wrongfully debarring him from the business and other accusations in relation to that.

I then had to suffer the discomfort of fronting up to a meeting with Wilson and our respective lawyers, where I had to sit through his lawyer accusing me of all sorts of wrongdoing. I sat there with my blood boiling, having been told by my lawyer to say nothing. My lawyer then advised that I had been acting on the direction of the ASC due to a matter pending against Wilson. He then invited Wilson's lawyer to a private chat in another room. I can only guess that he acquainted Wilson's lawyer with the facts because we never saw that lawyer again. After that, Wilson kept going from one lawyer to another.

One day, I was sitting in my office when Wilson arrived. He

came in and went straight to his office. He then came to me and said we needed to talk. I told him I had nothing whatsoever to say to him. He then proceeded to walk into Helen's office, demanded the bank books and then disappeared back into his office. He came out, threw the bank books onto Helen's desk and left. She was visibly shaken, but I had followed him and was ready to step in if he did anything untoward. He left, and we discovered that he had written himself a cheque.

From the outset of our joint venture, Wilson had continuously urged me to get rid of Helen as our bookkeeper, no doubt to put in place someone he could manipulate. Thank goodness I had steadfastly refused.

Then came the day when Wilson's committal trial was held at the Melbourne Magistrates' Court. Unbelievably, Wilson called me, Janine, and all the victims of his thefts as witnesses. He even called a sex worker in whose brothel he had invested a client's stolen money. It was not only bizarre, but it was also extremely stressful for his elderly clients, most of whom were from country towns outside of Melbourne. As the morning progressed, witnesses were called and simply confirmed that they had their money taken without permission.

I was called to testify just before lunch, and Wilson's lawyer proceeded to suggest that I knew what was going on and was somehow involved. The magistrate called a stop and asked the lawyer if that is what he was suggesting. He answered, 'That is how I have been briefed.' The magistrate lost it, called lunch recess and told Wilson's lawyer to go away and sort his client out.

As we gathered in the court lobby, we could hear Wilson's lawyer screaming at him somewhere else in the building. Following the lunch break, the magistrate refused to hear anymore and committed Wilson for trial.

We were treading water as far as the business went, engrossed with dealing with the loss claims of victims and nurturing them after this traumatic event. Obviously, we had to ensure that our client base who were not directly affected were assured that their affairs were safe, and we were looking after their wellbeing too. Of course, there were ongoing issues with Wilson, but he had quietened down since his committal to trial.

We started to get things back in order and back to some sense of normality when, in early 1993, Wilson finally appeared in court, still protesting his innocence. He had even convinced several people, including the principal of the private school that both our sons attended and a client of ours, to function as a character witness. How devastated he must have been when Wilson changed his plea to guilty at the courtroom door. Wilson was found guilty and given a prison sentence of three and a half years.

We celebrated the end to this nightmare, but in a cruel final blow, at the last minute we had to get Wilson to sign papers that would enable us to deregister the JV company and finally close the matter. As he waited at Pentridge Prison to be transported to his new abode, our lawyers were negotiating with him to agree to sign. In the end, we had to pay him $1,800 to sign. Just a final kick in the guts from my former partner.

I asked the fraud squad detectives how we could have guarded against this sort of thing happening. They said that in their experience, we had systems and protection mechanisms as good as they had ever seen, but if someone sets out to defraud, they will find a way, and it is almost impossible to stop. Having said that, we introduced new security measures to strengthen our cross-checking mechanisms.

The business aftermath

We had endured 18 months of hell. The stress was enormous and the pressure relentless. But as we reflected, we could now only celebrate the positives. Again, our core beliefs were the things that saved us. Our history of integrity, honesty and fair dealing resulted in the universal support of everyone we had dealings with – our clients, our professional networks, our licensee, our suppliers and our industry colleagues. Our attention to detail and pursuit of excellence, our innovation in the development of systems, and our record keeping all blended together not only to deal with the issues in an unbelievably efficient manner but to save us from what would have otherwise destroyed us.

Primarily, our systems, processes and record management saved the day. Our records were exemplary and applauded by all the investigators, auditors and police. We were able, with the help of Macquarie Bank Limited, to easily track all the illicit transactions and produce hard copy evidence. This also enabled the police to bring the matter to trial within 18 months, which was a record at that time.

I formed a close relationship with a senior partner at the PI company lawyers, Minter Ellison, and he employed me to provide expert opinion on PI insurance cases for years later. The fraud squad invited me, Janine and our two Macquarie

Bank assistants to their Christmas parties for years, and police and their family members became clients.

Most importantly, we were able to provide restitution to the injured clients via our PI insurance and provide them with the emotional support to put this dreadful experience behind them. In the interim, we established wonderfully close long-term relationships with them and with all, but one, remaining clients of the company.

We had survived the worst possible test and come out the other side triumphant. Our relationships across the board were now even stronger. It was clear that our clients and our colleagues had even more faith and trust in us, having witnessed firsthand how we had been able to protect the interests of our clients.

We were back on track and excited about the future. We started reviewing our systems and processes to see where we could improve and get back to our innovation mindset. The feeling was amazing.

Whilst our licensee, FPI, had been supportive of us, they were quick to protect themselves by auditing us and sending in their compliance team to review our files and processes. There was certainly a change in their attitude, and I could see that we needed to now apply for our own licence and part company with FPI.

As it happened, I had applied for a securities dealer licence for the JV company before the Wilson issues were discovered, and just a few days after the discovery, the ASC representative advised me that we had been successful, but I had to decline because of the issues unfolding. So, when I reapplied under our own corporate entity in 1993, the process was swift as the ASC was intimately aware of our history and how we had dealt with it.

Achieving an unrestricted securities dealer licence is complex and difficult to get. In our case, we also needed to be licensed to hold client securities at our address and obtain agency authority to operate their accounts. The ASC agreed with no further investigation.

We were now completely independent, so we were free to plan and control our own destiny in every sense. More celebrations!

If ever there was an ultimate test of systems and processes, this had to be it. I had to marvel at how, despite the worst thing that could happen to a financial management business, we survived with an enhanced reputation and widespread loyalties. It was unbelievable.

Oh, and I now never doubt my Helen's evaluation of people!

The personal aftermath

Unfortunately, I paid a heavy personal toll from this chapter in my life. I was no longer the same person as I was and had unknowingly suffered significant mental anguish, which became obvious after the event as the stress and the pressure of dealing with this disaster subsided.

I had developed a paranoid distrust of just about everyone and was prone to totally unreasonable outbursts when I thought that anyone had betrayed my trust or acted against my principles. Sadly, the victims were usually those closest to me, which I deeply regret to this day. This soon became a problem that I could not ignore, and I sought professional help, which sadly was of absolutely no help at all. Fortunately, Helen and our children, Sarah and Andrew, gathered around me, and we resolved how to deal with my paranoia between us.

I thought I had this issue under control, but in later years it surfaced again from time to time, and, eventually, I had to do some serious soul searching to deal with it. I don't think I will ever completely cure this problem, but it certainly has subsided since I retired and became de-stressed.

I share this as I think people in business tend to consider themselves as being 'bulletproof' when it comes to stress-related issues. I was left in no doubt of the stress I had been carrying about, probably for my entire business career, when I experienced the relief from the enormous weight of stress the moment I retired. Whilst much of this can be attributed to historic traumatic events, I have no doubt that some of it was simply due to the burden of responsibility of running a business.

Chapter 9

Investment philosophy and innovation

1988–1994

Note: despite the distraction of the Wilson saga from 1991–1993, Janine and I had proceeded to develop our new portfolio management systems and processes in the wake of the 1987 stock market crash, infamously known as 'Black Monday'. Firstly in conjunction with FPI, which was initially launched in late 1988 and then refined into our wholly internal system launched in 1994.

n the wake of the 1987 stock market crash, my innovative juices were running wild. The more I considered what had happened and why, I could not help but think there had to be a better way to manage money, protect the clients' interests and have the flexibility to take advantage of market volatility. I worked out a set of basic portfolio strategy requirements, then Janine and I started working on the development of an alternative client management platform which would operate more efficiently and cost-effectively.

Our new securities licensee FPI had already been supportive of our customisation of their management software in conjunction with their software programmers, which was helpful. Of course, we knew that they would make use of our ideas to help further enhance their model, but that was okay. We then designed our own spreadsheets to enable us to do customised reporting.

We now had progressed our software development to the point where we could prepare to implement. It was extremely exciting as it would provide our clients with a far more attractive and efficient management system at a reduced cost. It would also result in us assuming control of our clients' affairs entirely and independently of any external provider. The clients would have complete ownership and control of their investments.

The six bases for our model were:

1. Investments would be made in the clients' name and addressed to the care of our office for administration purposes. This would dispense with the need for an expensive trustee company and give the clients comfort of outright ownership of their assets. With the clients' assets addressed to care of our office, we would deal with all their assets, correspondence, income management and banking. In other words, we managed everything on their behalf in-house.

2. The central plank of the client's account would be a client-owned cash management account through which all transactions – buys, sells, income, and payments – would be made. This would effectively enable us to balance the clients' portfolio against the bank account daily, thus providing accuracy, security and client peace of mind.

3. We would invest directly into investment markets, such as ASX-listed shares, bank-backed debentures and ASX-listed property trusts. Where we could not gain access to direct markets, we would use selected managed

funds but under strict criteria. This would give clients absolute control over their destiny regardless of market movements, enable the flexibility to take advantage of strategic opportunities and control over cash flows.

4. We would be completely fee-based and aim to provide a state-of-the-art service at a reasonable cost.

     • (Note: the financial industry at that time was entirely commission-based with advisers being paid obscene levels of commissions for placing clients' money into managed investments.)

5. We would use FPI software and a series of spreadsheets we designed to manage everything in-house. This meant we could instantly respond to client queries and requests on a daily basis.

6. By cutting out layers of cost, we could virtually halve the client management fee cost and become more profitable than previously.

This was highly innovative and like nothing that existed in the market at the time and remains unique today. Comparatively, it is an extremely high-touch and time-consuming process, which our competitors would shun. But our differential was our systems innovation, which we were positive that over time we could design to become so efficient that it would be extremely cost-effective.

By late 1988, we were ready to launch, and the client reaction was sensational. Not only did it give them the elements of ownership and security they craved, but they could understand it and appreciate how it worked. They loved the fact that they could get instant action and responses direct from us and understood the management of their cashflows. Obviously, it had an astounding effect on the development of our client relationships and brought us all closer together in partnership.

We had established a relationship with Macquarie Bank, which operated a cash management trust. They were particularly good to deal with, and we developed a remarkably close relationship. Together we developed a system where they would provide a courier each night to collect our daily banking. The next morning, they would deliver cheques and transaction reports summarising the transactions for the day. This was long before the days of data downloads, so it was a manual process.

Macquarie Bank had only obtained a banking licence in 1986, so it was in its infancy. They were keen and more flexible in their approach to dealing with niche markets. Janine and I brainstormed the issue of manual bank data entry and came up with the bright idea that Macquarie could put our clients' daily bank transactions on a computer floppy disc and we could get FPI to program a data matching system, which they did. This initiative was an early version of data transfer, and it worked a treat, making our job easier and faster with increased efficiency.

We contracted our investment research and secured daily market price updates, so we were close to having real-time portfolio updates available to our clients. We continued to provide hard copy reports to our clients on a quarterly basis, but they knew they could call us anytime and obtain updated information. This was in the late 1980s, when we had no internet.

Our quarterly reporting at the time consisted of a folder with portfolio reports, research documents and a lengthy market report. We surveyed our clients regularly for feedback, and one of the major things they told us was that they were not interested in anything other than their portfolio reports and a cash statement. This was great for us but led to more innovation later.

Together with Macquarie, we developed system enhancements that increased the automation of data transfer and other innovative system developments. More efficiency through innovation.

The wonderful thing about this system was that it was live, based on real-time cash movements, and we had total control over our clients' affairs whilst all the assets and accounts remained registered in their name. Thus, clients had total control over their destiny and access to information. We could predict cash flows based on current rates and plot cash flows so we could manage client incomes very accurately.

We designed a system where all client interfaces were recorded on their electronic file. So, if they called and their regular contact was not available, anyone could take the call, refer to the notes in the system and provide an instant response.

Our core values were our drivers again, and the innovation piece was exhilarating. Over the years, we continued to innovate and enhance our systems so that they became a total practice management system providing extraordinary efficiencies and functionalities.

The adaptation of the FPI software, however, was an interim solution and had its shortcomings that were frustrating. We surveyed the market to try and find an existing solution but could not find anything that achieved our desired outcomes. The closest was HiPortfolio, the system used by the banking industry, but this was based on assumptive dividend reporting, not factual, so it was of no use to our cash-based model and our need for real-time reporting.

From a business structure point of view, I have a strong view that ownership of data is essential. As soon as the control of corporate data and intellectual property, in respect to how that data is managed and ownership of the management software is outsourced, the company loses control and is subject to risk. In addition, a company that has complete control and ownership of its data and how it is managed is a great deal more valuable than one who is dependent on external providers.

The ability to customise and react to recognised opportunities for business enhancement is a massive benefit and market advantage. The use of proprietary systems, that is, those designed for a broad industry need, will always be compromised to some extent and designed to suit basic or generic demands, with little or no opportunity for customisation.

My early learning on the ownership of data came about five years into our journey with the development of our own internal portfolio administration IT system (discussed more later on). I asked the programmer who owned the source codes of the program, and, to my dismay, he told me he owned them. He said he had asked me at the outset if I intended on selling the system, and I replied that I did not. He took that as meaning that he retained control of the systems source codes and could license or sell them off to others at his will, and he had priced his services accordingly on that basis. This was clearly not acceptable to me, and it cost me $170,000 to buy the source codes off him for a system that we had designed in finite detail and for which he had simply written the code (and had been paid well to do so).

Anyone who has ventured into the development of software will know how frustrating it is. IT developers specialise in making the simple complicated but are notoriously unreliable in respect to meeting deadlines. I have a firm view that to control the process and manage it as effectively as possible, it is essential that the users dictate the terms. It is the users who understand the processes and the required result. It is not necessary to understand programming, just the process and the desired outcome. Once the database is established, it is a matter of developing transaction types, their characteristics and basic mathematical formulas to dictate the character of the transaction. Making it pretty is up to the designer. When you think about it, a computer programmer knows little about a business or how it works, so it is vital to explain it as clearly as humanly possible and ignore the programmers attempts at blinding you with technical jargon and the perceived complexity of IT development. In our experience, after we gained an understanding of the process, we finished up writing a large amount of the coding formulas ourselves, as it was easier than trying to explain it to the programmer.

Contrary to most companies' views, we automate everything that is repetitive to achieve optimum efficiency and reduce the chance of human error. We do not automate to reduce people. We want our people to have more face-to-face time with our clients and build relationships. The result is that our team develops great personal relationships, which generates greater satisfaction all around.

Chapter 10

Market crises and investment philosophy

We have experienced market crises, starting for me with the 1987 stock market crash. Then came the 1990 banking crisis, impacting both property and share markets; the property market crash of the mid-90s; the bond market crash of 1995; the Asian share market collapse of 1998; the 'tech wreck' share market crash of 2000; the 9/11 US terrorist attacks of 2001, which impacted share markets globally; and the Global Financial Crisis of 2007–2009, which had ramifications for share markets, property markets and debt securities. Most recently, we had the COVID-19 pandemic of 2020–2021, which caused a short-term reaction to share markets. All these presented challenges, and whilst we did not always get it entirely right, we had the portfolio strategy, the structure and the systems, and the ability to be proactive with the flexibility to protect our clients' interests and take advantage of the opportunities that always arise from a market crisis.

The investment industry is laden with all sorts of market-based theories and schemes that product manufacturers love to use. There is this obsession with these theoretical bases for market movements or investment strategies that mesmerises many, and it seems the more complex the better. In reality, most consumers have no idea. Over the years, I have attended countless conferences around the world and listened to so-called expert commentators spruiking their theories, and I just scratch my head in dismay.

I recall attending a conference in the US where a renowned diversification theorist was a key speaker. He gave a presentation that claimed that regardless of any other consideration, diversification across all sectors, regardless of market conditions, would always outperform any other strategy. He presented complex tables, illustrating his point that even when the worst-performing asset sectors were included, his theory would outperform. This seemed illogical to me, until I studied his tables later to find that he had conveniently used different date ranges for different asset classes, which completely biased the outcome in his favour.

I took a simplistic and pragmatic view of effective investment theory, and it is broadly based on Warren Buffett's beliefs of intrinsic value and long-term strategy. It is also based on designing an investment portfolio strategy to achieve specific outcomes in line with the client's financial objectives.

The efficient market theory espouses that share market prices are an efficient reflection of value. Of course, this is true in respect to the rules of supply and demand but nonsense in respect to the reflection of intrinsic value, as whilst share prices can be affected by short-term external influences that affect their market price, it has nothing to do with their intrinsic (or true) value.

Fear and greed also drive the markets. Fear when share prices fall and greed when prices rise. This results in investors panicking when markets fall, so they sell when prices are low. When markets rally, investors get excited and buy when prices are high. This is particularly true in times of extraordinary events such as the 9/11 terrorist attacks and the COVID-19 pandemic.

Investors panicked primarily over the fear of the unknown. I take the view that cool logic supports the view that mankind will always be driven to survive and continue to consume goods and services no matter what. Therefore, economies and markets will always rebound from short-term influences.

Our approach would utilise intrinsic value-based research and other assessment criteria, including dividend value. We would only include shares that were market leaders and had the capacity to deliver client outcomes.

Asset allocation, that is, determining a client's portfolio strategy in terms of the types and quantity of investment types, would be our starting point. But we would determine this by an analysis of the client's financial requirements, both short and long term, and then designing a portfolio mix that would achieve the desired outcomes. Once this strategy had been determined, it would remain unchanged unless the client circumstances required it or market movements effected the percentage asset balance as illustrated by the graph below.

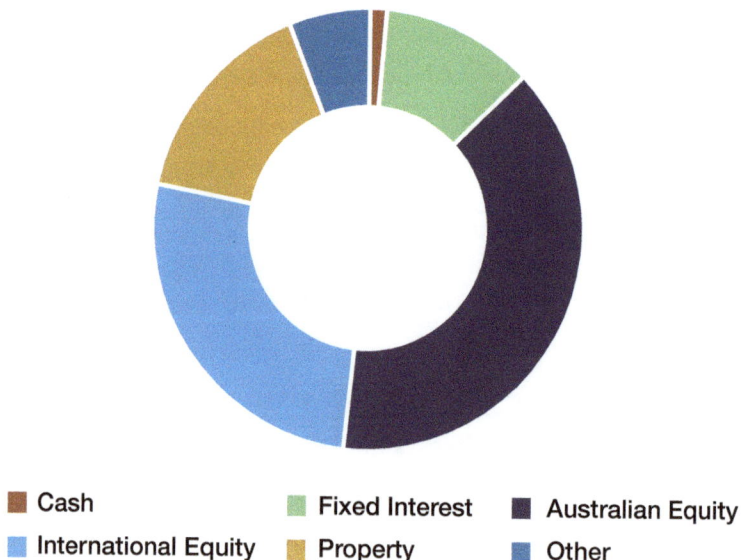

■ Cash   ■ Fixed Interest   ■ Australian Equity
■ International Equity   ■ Property   ■ Other

Our portfolio management tool would be a disciplined rebalance mechanism that we could manage efficiently and act quickly on market trends or share fluctuations where necessary. The way rebalancing works is that, when markets move out of sync with each other or individual investments outperform, it will typically impact the asset allocation compared to the model. This balance would be regularly monitored so that if a client's asset allocation became unbalanced compared to the plan, we would reduce the outperforming class and rebalance over the classes. This has the effect of selling high and buying low and keeping faith with the strategic plan and its outcomes..

When markets suffer an extraordinary downturn for some reason, we see this as a prime opportunity to rebalance, buying quality assets at a discounted price, which provides capital gain upside and dividend growth opportunities.

We took the view that in times of adversity, we had the chance to prove our worth by getting on the front foot and acting to achieve remarkable results, manage our clients' immediate concerns and provide peace of mind. Our strategies locked in cash flows, and that alone gave clients comfort, knowing that their income streams remained intact, regardless of a fall in market values.

But the most important thing in times of crisis is communication. We were fast and active in communicating with our clients both through general written commentary and individual personal contact. Because of our investment philosophies and portfolio structuring, we could take a positive approach, provide reassurance and act.

I distinctly remember the 2000 'tech wreck', when the technology sector had become overpriced and crashed spectacularly. Leading up to this, IT was the flavour of the month for the managed fund industry, with tech funds flooding the market. The financial planning community had overinvested their clients' money in these high-risk funds, and when the market plunged, people got hurt. At about this time, my colleagues and I attended a financial planning conference in Sydney, which was attended by financial planning principles from Australia and around the world. It was astounding to us that so many of the advisers that attended had advised their clients to overweight their investments in this sector. What was more astounding was that advisers were refusing to answer their panicking clients' telephone calls and many advisers present at the conference were in tears.

Another prime example of flavour of the month investing was 'BRIC' (an acronym for Brazil, Russia, India and China). The term BRIC, coined in 2001, was originally identified to highlight investment opportunities based on a theory that these countries would outperform the traditional Western-led countries of the world over the ensuing decades. What followed was a proliferation of BRIC investment funds and the usual sheep-like trend for advisers to recommend them. In 2009, the BRICS organisation, which started off as an informal group of countries, was formed into an intergovernmental organisation and was expanded to include other countries in the years to follow.

Based on experience, we had a policy that we would only invest in the quality end of key markets and would gain exposure to specialist markets via large corporations. So rather than invest in high-risk BRIC funds, we invested via direct share exposure in the US and selected wholesale managed funds that would provide access to similar companies that were physically developing their company exposure to the BRIC economies. What transpired was that our clients benefitted from the growth experienced by these huge companies, which resided in well-regulated markets like the US, whilst the BRIC markets collapsed after the Global Financial Crisis of 2007–2008.

This was yet another example of running with the managed fund herd and failing to have a client-focused approach to portfolio construction. We had minimal exposure to these funds, not because we were wiser than anyone else in evaluating them; we just had a disciplined approach to investment for each individual client and a policy to avoid being caught up in short-term 'themes' of investment.

The 9/11 terrorist attacks on the US and the COVID-19 market corrections were quite different from all the others as they related to specific external events and were not market-related as such. The result was the same in respect to emotionally driven market reactions, but there was no fundamental market or economic weakness involved.

Philosophically speaking, the world is a giant marketplace that constantly consumes goods and services. Demand for goods and services will fluctuate regardless of market conditions. But the overriding reality is that we must consume to survive. So, there is no other outcome possible from a major market downturn than recovery, so I suggest that the risk of buying high-quality assets in a downturn is a minimal-risk, high-return strategy.

Fear of the unknown is a key market driver and results in continuing market fluctuations from things like government elections and impending announcements such as interest rates. But in the case of 9/11 and COVID-19, it was the fear of the unknown resulting from extraordinary events that caused the markets to correct. We took the view that this was purely emotion-driven and an excellent opportunity to invest, as the correction was bound to recover quickly as acceptance and calmness returned.

The Global Financial Crisis (GFC) of 2007 was the worst of all the corrections that occurred during my time (since the 1987 crash) and had a profound effect on my younger colleagues. There were distinct differences in that it was due to a global underlying weakness in financial systems and had a disastrous impact on many countries around the world, with some like Greece, Ireland and Italy coming close to economic collapse.

The GFC was particularly difficult, as it took around three years to recover value, and the ASX-200 only recovered to its pre-GFC levels in 2023. In the meantime, there were victims with companies going into liquidation, and with the weakness in the banking sector, a squeeze on credit.

Of particular concern, was the impact of short selling on the ASX. Short selling is when an institutional investor, like a hedge fund, will attack a company by using borrowed shares to aggressively sell massive quantities of shares. This can cause a sharp fall in market value, at which point the short seller buys the shares back at a cheap price, repays the loan and pockets the difference.

My pet hate is short selling, as it is purely market manipulation and not in the interest of investors or a fair market. Numerous movies have been made featuring short selling dramas, including true stories depicted in *The Big Short* and *The Wolf of Wall Street*. Whilst on holiday on a sea cruise, I got talking to a gentleman who had been a member of the ASX board. I asked for his opinion on short selling, and he nearly choked. He said he abhorred the practice and had approached the chair of the ASX at the time and proposed it should be banned. The chair told him that would never happen as the ASX made too much money from the practice. So much for a fair market – too many snouts in the trough.

In specific cases, the sharp decline in a share's price caused by short selling can trigger other consequences, like the breach of a loan covenant, which can and did send companies into liquidation, causing innocent investors unnecessary loss.

We had to work extremely hard through the GFC to ensure that our clients understood this drawn-out market downturn and pursued rebalancing opportunities to take advantage of purchasing undervalued shares. Most important was our ability to reassure clients that despite any fall in value of investments, their portfolio income was unaffected so that, in the short term, there was nothing to worry about.

Once again, our proactive initiative-taking approach and close client relationships enabled us to survive and reap the benefits on behalf of our clients. Our portfolios held up well, but they were not immune from a fall in value, which was unavoidable; however, we were easily able to explain our strategy, and the clients understood and were comfortable.

During the GFC, we gained an influx of new clients who had been dissatisfied with their former advisers. But the business suffered financially as our fees are related to portfolio values, which had reduced in line with the market correction. We had always taken the view that if the client's fund value falls, so too should our fees. This was appreciated by our clients at these times.

The GFC caused massive staff retrenchments throughout the financial sector, and although we ran at a small loss for one year and had to review our overall position, we determined that we did not want to lose any of our team members. We resolved to offer them the opportunity to reduce their hours and salary by 10% for the sake of everyone retaining their jobs. This applied to everyone, including me and my senior colleagues. Everyone enthusiastically agreed, and that is what we did. As it happened after six months, we restored everyone to full-time hours.

The reaction of our people was quite amazing and humbling. Many of them came to me and thanked me for allowing them to be part of the solution to hold the team together. Some took a 10% pay cut but still worked full time. After the panic died down and we got back to near normal, we celebrated together, and no doubt, our culture was even stronger.

Today we love market corrections, and so do our clients. They know that it is a chance for opportunity when, to quote Warren Buffet, 'A simple rule dictates my buying: be fearful when others are greedy and be greedy when others are fearful'. Or, to quote Winston Churchill, 'Never let a good crisis go to waste'.

Clare Blizzard, my EA for over 20 years – the clients loved her

Chris Morcom, my first equity partner, presenting at the staff retreat, 2024

The Hewison & Associates office in Howitt Street,
South Yarra from 1996 to 2002

My first group of young equity partners – Chris Morcom,
Andrew Hewison, Nathan Lear, Glenn Fairbairn, Simon
Curtain (clockwise from left), c. 2005

Janine 'I don't do figures' Gordon.
A great contributor to the
foundation of HPW

Long-term Practice
Manager Effie Goumas

Helen and me in the early days, c. 1990

Glenn, Chris, John and Andrew at the
AFR Asset Magazine Awards, 2006

Glenn, Clare, me and Chris talking strategy, c. 2005

HPW equity partners in 2014 (l–r) – Andrew, Nathan Lear,
me, Simon, Chris and Glenn

New partners Pierce Hanlon (r) and Travis Schindler (l)
with Andrew and Simon

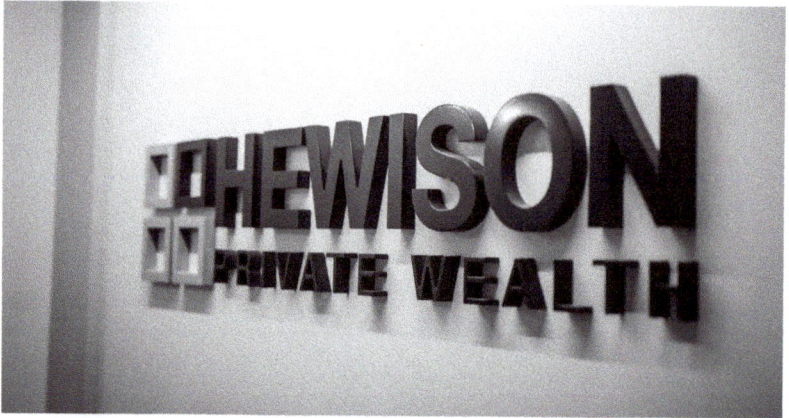

The HPW 4 pillars logo – Integrity, Innovation, Expertise and Independence

Catching up in the staff room for a chat

The HPW team at the staff retreat, 2024

A staff retreat session, 2024

Front of house superstar Leonnie Colwell

Handing over the HPW reins to Andrew

PART 2

My core beliefs

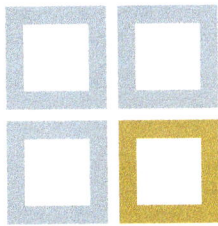

Chapter 11

Integrity and relationship values

I was determined to establish a business of the highest integrity and develop close relationships with our clients, suppliers and professional colleagues based on trust and mutual respect. This was important to me as a matter of principle but also to building the image of the business in the longer term.

Integrity not only applies to honesty, ethical and moral standards and fair dealing but also to the development of strong long-term relationships, both internal and external.

I guess my attitude towards fair dealing came from my parents, who always preached the virtues of honesty and fair dealing, often quoting the Bible verse 'Do to others as you would have them do to you' from Luke 6:31. This relates to treating others with kindness, respect and empathy and was further reinforced by my mentors, Geoff Brash and Rob Roberts, who were both sticklers for upholding these standards.

I am a bit of a zealot when it comes to upholding ideals. Over the years, I have often been admonished by my colleagues and friends for refusing to take advantage of opportunities to bend the rules, no matter how trivial, when it comes to obtaining an undeserved advantage at someone else's expense. It's a bit like cheating at golf, as my father used to say, 'the only person you are cheating is yourself'.

I learnt at an early age that building trusting relationships with people, in all walks of life, depended upon truth and loyalty. Like most of us, I was guilty of telling some porkies as a young man trying to impress, but as I matured, I learnt that most people had excellent intuition and could usually see through exaggerations and untruths. I developed the habit of always telling the truth, and I now find it virtually impossible to do otherwise.

I firmly believe that long-term relationships in business rely heavily on the principle of honesty, fairness, empathy and trust.

One aspect of this principle relates to fair dealing with our suppliers. I saw it as a responsibility of ours to treat people with respect in every aspect of our dealings, particularly in meeting our obligation to pay our bills on time. At the time, it was common practice for many businesses to stretch their creditors from the standard 30-day payment terms to 60 or 90 days. This was typical of big business' treatment of their smaller suppliers.

I had friends in business that had suffered constantly from delayed payments, which meant they effectively had to fund their operations on debt caused by the non-payment of their creditors. I found this practice to be abhorrent and grossly unfair and often resulted in small businesses being forced to close due to an inability to fund their creditors. In the building industry, it was very common for construction companies to simply close, owing vast sums to suppliers, and then open under another entity the next day.

I recall a friend of mine, who owned a cabinet-making business, telling me that this had happened to him. A builder client who owed his business a large amount of money, outstanding over 90 days, had closed his business due to insolvency. The builder reopened under a different entity and, shortly after, had the gall to wave to my friend as he drove past him in his Porsche.

I admit being paranoid about the matter of account payments, and we always paid our bills on time or early. As I mentioned earlier in the book, this saved us later when our backs were against the wall and our suppliers supported us.

Ethical behaviour is a non-negotiable aspect in any business, but especially so in a professional business such as ours that deals with people's money. It was important for me to create an atmosphere where ethical behaviour was constantly front of mind in all of our dealings and decision-making processes. I found it interesting that in our ethics training sessions, it was sometimes difficult to determine what was the appropriate ethical decision in some complex scenarios. My point being, it is not sufficient to just claim to behave ethically, it requires education, understanding and attention to detail.

One example of ethical behaviour occurred when I was Brash's product manager for home entertainment products, reporting to the director in charge, who had virtually no experience in the field. The incident began when my then boss visited a supplier and undertook to purchase a quantity of top-end hi-fi speakers. He did not seek my opinion or advice on this purchase, and it was just before I left Brash to join Norlin. I was later to learn that after the first delivery batch of the speakers, the salespeople in the Brash's retail stores rejected them out of hand as being inferior to other brands and more expensive. My former boss reacted by cancelling the rest of the order, leaving the supplier holding a quantity of product they could not sell elsewhere.

The owner of the business telephoned Geoff Brash at his home and told him the story. The next day, Geoff demanded that the agreement be honoured and the order be reinstated. Geoff was livid, as his principles of honour and fair dealing had been contravened. I subsequently heard from my Norlin boss, Rob Roberts, that Geoff

Brash had confided in him that my former boss had blamed me for recommending the speakers and approving the order. This, of course, was a complete fabrication aimed at covering his backside, and I was enraged at this insult to my integrity.

As it happened, Rob and I were in Chicago attending a Norlin function, as were Geoff and Jenny Brash. They invited us to join them for dinner at their hotel, specifically to get my side of the story regarding this incident. I enlightened Geoff with the facts pertaining to the matter and was relieved when he told me that he had doubts about the veracity of the explanation he had been given and accepted my version of events. I took this as a confirmation of his trust and later learnt that my former boss had been terminated.

Relationships were one of the keys to our business' success on every level. We focused on making every member of our team feel like a member of the 'family'. We treated our relationships with our professional colleagues and our suppliers as vitally important to the structure of our business, and over time this has proven to be the case. We have experienced an extraordinary advantage from the close connections we have formed, which have delivered significant benefits to our development over the years.

Of course, the relationships we shared with our clients were the most important factor in our business success. Again, we set out to develop close, lifelong relationships and work in partnership with our clients to achieve the outcomes they desired and some they couldn't have imagined. We welcomed them as members of our family, and I treasure the relationships I formed with my clients over the years, which have now transcended into close friendships I still enjoy despite my retirement from the business.

These factors are the absolute basis of the character of our business and a huge contributor to our success. I have no doubt that the reputation we have built over the years has resulted in major advantages to the business generally, and to our clients, as we became a preferred business partner with quality organisations that only dealt with selected business partners. This is particularly true in the realm of prestige investment managers, who only deal with a select elite level of distributors with a high-quality client base. We enjoy many such relationships from which our clients have derived substantial financial benefit through exclusive access to high-quality investment opportunities.

Chapter 12

Innovation and change

love change and innovation. I constantly look for opportunities for change and better ways to do things. It is just ingrained in my DNA, and it gives me the greatest buzz to initiate change and stay ahead of the pack.

One of my aims in life is to learn something new every day. I do not consciously go looking for new things, but it is certainly embedded in my subconscious mind, and when I see or hear something that gives me an 'aha' moment, I recognise it and commit it to memory.

I have learnt over the years to be a great listener. Everyone has wisdom, and I listen intently to everyone no matter their age, occupation or status in life; I listen and learn. Sometimes I learn things I need to guard against, opinions that I may not agree with but need to be taken into consideration, or things that are truly mind changing. It does not matter what it is; it is worth knowing. But often I pick up real gems that manifest into great ideas for innovation.

I feel sorry for people who think they know it all or refuse to consider another point of view, as they are robbing themselves of broadening their knowledge or missing an opportunity for change.

Innovation is one of the keys to success as it concentrates on new and improved ways of doing things, which, from a business sense, maintains its energy and currency, and its competitive edge. In life, it keeps me constantly invigorated and forward thinking.

From the very start, our business plan was laced with innovative ideas on management techniques, systemic change and the pursuit of excellence. I get excited just thinking about it.

I used to attend conferences both in Australia and around the world looking for innovative ideas and initiatives or new innovations, particularly in IT systems. I invariably came away with the latest ideas but counted it as a win if I just satisfied myself that we were ahead of the game.

I attended the Financial Planning Association of Australia (FPA) annual conference in 1992, which consisted of three days of plenary and technical sessions. One of the sessions was presented by a financial planner from the US who ran a small practice but had designed and developed their own software, which operated in a comparable manner to us. I immediately decided that based on the spreadsheets and processes we already had in place, we could do the same thing. I discussed it with Janine, who became just as excited as me.

We contacted a programmer, who I knew from my days with Beyson, that already had existing knowledge of portfolio software. We gave him a strict and specific brief on what we wanted to achieve, down to the number of keystrokes we wanted for each transaction and to get from one screen to another.

In 1993, having returned to a form of normality post Wilson, we were now effectively relaunching with a newfound enthusiasm and drive. We had a staff of five people: me, Janine (now as operations manager), a client services manager, a secretary/receptionist and Helen as bookkeeper. We had our own securities dealer licence, so we were now masters of our own destiny and completely independent.

It took us until early 1994 to develop our portfolio management system, ready for launch. I recall I was at an external meeting as Janine and the programmer loaded the software. I received a phone call from Janine to tell me the entire system had crashed, and they were trying to retrieve all our historic information. Oh, the joys of IT development! Later in the day, the problems were corrected and the system launched successfully. We called it PA for 'Portfolio Administration' – a humble name for what was a revolutionary system.

So, from the horrific experience of the stock market crash came inspiration and innovation, turning the 'lemon into lemonade'. Now we could deliver our clients a far superior service on every level, achieve a tailored investment strategy delivering client control and flexibility, reliability and predictability of cash flows and immediate access to information. The clients just loved the outcomes we were now able to deliver. We had gone from providing six-week-old portfolio reporting to portfolio data updates every 24 hours and ASX pricing updates daily and others pricing fortnightly. The cash account was accurate and updated daily. This was all revolutionary, particularly bearing in mind we were restricted to old-fashioned communication by floppy disc downloads, courier services and facsimile transmissions. No internet, no online data feeds, no websites.

We continued to constantly develop PA and our other systems. We had a policy that said, 'if a process or transaction occurs multiple times, it must be automated.' So, we just continued to improve our efficiency over time.

Progressively, we enhanced the capability of PA to become a full-blown practice management system that incorporated extraordinary time savings, efficiency and enhanced service delivery. Apart from the efficient management of client portfolios, some of the key elements were:

- Customer success management (CSM): This included all the client's personal background and contact details, including personal information like family members, likes and dislikes, important dates, etc. This fed into actions to help us make the customer experience more personal and enjoyable.

- Financial planning processing: This tracked and monitored every step of the transaction process, from implementation of the initial account set-up, portfolio construction and continuous reviews and actions. This ensured that processes were monitored and efficiently implemented.

- Investment portfolio construction: This enabled the planners to design portfolios within the system incorporating the asset allocation balance and the selection from the current list of authorised investments. It would then manage the process from client approval to the purchase of investment and finalisation of the operational piece of the overall strategy plan.

- Portfolio management: This allowed for regular client portfolios to be reviewed and scheduled and reminders generated. The system provided for the rebalance of portfolios in line with the strategic plan. It also enabled the review of all clients holding a specific investment that we wanted to review.

- Compliance mechanisms: This programmed compliance mechanisms within the processes of our IT systems so that effectively, the system would not allow a transaction to proceed unless it fell within the compliance boundaries. In this way, compliance became efficient, effective and relatively inexpensive. Compliance is the common enemy of the financial planning community. It is generally thought to be too complex, time-consuming and expensive. I have always taken the opposite view and believe that compliance with regulatory standards is just good housekeeping and protects the client's interest.

- Taxation management and reporting: This allowed us, to the extent possible, to apply income tax rates to the investments so that we could forecast taxation outcomes and maintain capital gains tax. As we managed all the income to the client portfolio, we maintained most of the tax information and supporting documentation to provide the client's accountant with comprehensive tax reporting at year end. We also had our systems audited so we could provide an audit letter to the accountant confirming the accuracy of the data.

- Automation of multiple transactions and data uploads: This provided efficiency with handling bulk transactions such as corporate actions requiring client acceptance or rejection of an offer such as a bonus issue or share buy-back. These matters were often time-sensitive, requiring fast processing. Data uploads from various sources added enormous efficiency and prompt client access to information.

We became well known throughout the industry as an innovator and market leader in what later became known as Individually Managed Accounts (IMAs). I was called upon to present at conferences around Australia and overseas in the US, India and Japan.

Over the years, we have constantly reviewed our business and developed an atmosphere of innovation and change to a point where it has become baked into our DNA. The constant focus is on how we can improve, how we can innovate to retain our leading edge, how we can achieve more efficiency through innovation, and how we can ramp up our client service offering. If you walked into our office, those are the conversations you would hear – every day. The company has now embarked on a complete system re-engineering as PA's technology has become outdated. We quickly discovered that there was still no existing comparative system to match our model, so it has been a considerable task to redevelop.

Working in this atmosphere of engagement and creativity is simply electric and incredibly motivating and exciting. You can feel it in the air. And I loved being surrounded by young people who were smarter than me and exhilarated by the excitement of change, innovation and the pursuit of excellence.

The systems we created in the late 1980s enabled us to provide a complete financial management service to our clients. We provided professional strategic advice, then put the strategy in place under our stewardship. We were available to them 24/7 and looked after their every need.

We developed our website at the end of 1998, which was within 6 months of Australia being connected to the internet. As we launched our website, we thought of the idea of enabling clients to access their portfolio data via our website. Our developer got to work, and to our knowledge, we were the first financial services business in Australia to offer online portfolio access to its clients.

We have continued to develop online access over the years and now provide clients with the ability to access a whole raft of current information on their financial affairs and portfolio analysis.

In the early 2000s, the latest development in financial planning coming out of the US were Individually Managed Accounts, or IMAs (as mentioned earlier), which revolutionised the financial planning industry. An IMA is an administration platform that advisers can use for managing their clients' investments and for which they can charge a fee. They are typically quite restrictive in respect to the mix and nature of investments they enable advisers to use and lack flexibility. These were a sort of institutionalised version of what we have been doing for more than a decade. These days, IMAs are mainly based on a suite of model portfolios that are characterised by a strategic outcome like income or growth. This is typical of the industry's habit of packaging processes into marketable products for broad circulation.

The major differences between our offering and IMAs were that we designed bespoke portfolio strategies based on individual client outcomes and circumstances using a wide range of direct market investments and wholesale funds. We also worked hard on the client relationship and did all the work on the clients' behalf. It was not difficult for us to keep innovating and stay well ahead of our competitors in this space. In fact, to this day, we do not know anyone in Australia who offers the breadth of service that we do.

We continue to redevelop systems to provide more efficiency through automated processes and lines of communication. Our aims are to achieve improved service delivery and reduce costs through greater efficiency. We do not aim to reduce people; we aim to enable them to spend more time in client-facing activity building relationships.

Chapter 13

Independence and conflicts of interest

1994

I ndependence and the elimination of conflicts of interest are key requirements to the delivery of fiduciary duty, which is essential in a professional advice and client relationship. Under the government regulations, a licensee may only claim independence if it can demonstrate a complete absence of any conflicts of interest.

Independence was also an essential element of our business plan. As I mentioned earlier, when I started out, most financial planners earned their income from commissions generated by financial product manufacturers or major financial institutions. The financial institutions saw financial planners as their sales force.

I could never come to grips with this concept. It was my view that financial planning was an advice-based profession, and the investment products were simply tools used as part of strategy delivery. So, independence became a vital element of our business model, as did fee-based advice with no commissions. We made this transition incredibly early on and gained full independence in 1993 when we obtained a securities dealer licence.

Historically, the financial services industry has a terrible history of questionable practices, shonky schemes, institutional rip-offs and overpricing. It has had multilayered structures of self-interest and 'snouts in the trough', resulting in outrageous costs to clients. To illustrate, a client could be charged 5% just for the privilege of placing funds with an institution. The adviser who recommended the product would earn a commission of 4%. Then there could be up to a 1% per annum service fee, commonly called 'trailing commissions', paid to the adviser just for leaving the money with the institution. Then there would be a fee for a portfolio administration platform with more kickbacks to the adviser.

In 1994, I was a speaker at the annual FPA conference in Melbourne, attended by 3,000 financial planners from around the world. My presentation was about independence and fee-based advice. There was a high attendance, which was generally supportive of the views I expressed. But I was surprised by some of the post-conference reactions from my detractors. I received threatening and sometimes abusive telephone calls from commission-based advisers and negative comments from a few institutional executives that utilised the commission model. I found this quite amusing at the time and indicative that I had managed to ruffle some feathers.

The corporate industry model was referred to as 'vertical integration', where the corporate entity controlled every function of the service offering, from the licence, and the advice, to the product manufacture, supply and account management. Then add ancillary services like life insurance and banking. There was a price applicable to every stage of this process, making it outrageously expensive to the client for a seriously inadequate service or value-add.

Our model was simple. We charged for preparing the client's comprehensive advice document. We did not charge anything for funds invested. Our clients' investments consisted predominantly of direct market securities, as distinct from managed funds, so there was no commission. Where we did need to use product, it would be wholesale where there are no commissions, or we would rebate any commission paid to us back to the client. Then we charged an annual fee for the complete administration of a client's affairs and continuing advice for a nominal cost of less than 1% per annum, which was tax deductible to the client.

Independence was key to the service offering, which was totally client-focused with no relationship with any external institution. The client had to have peace of mind that our only relationship was with them and our sole motivator was their best interests. We had no personal stake whatsoever in the investments we chose for our clients, so they could be completely comfortable that our advice was unbiased.

My senior management experience through working for a public company like Brash Holdings taught me much about how major corporates work and their key drivers. In the case of publicly listed companies, they are subject to constant scrutiny of their performance and their current market status with respect to profit and the balance sheet. I had been invited to attend board meetings at Brash and saw firsthand how sensitive the board was to these issues. These days it is even more critical as information is available much faster and companies are evaluated on ridiculously short timeframes.

I have long argued that professional advice cannot be corporatised. We have seen efforts by consolidators to use ASX-listed vehicles to corporatise accountants, doctors and lawyers. All have failed due to the fact that there is no margin for corporate profits in a professional model, and the drivers for both are entirely different. Listed corporations are driven by profit, and professions are driven by client fiduciary duty and the value of their advice, and they charge accordingly. Placing professional advice within a corporate hierarchy structure simply does not work.

In recent years, we have seen enormous controversy over the unacceptable practices of corporately owned financial planning businesses in Australia, in particular the big banks. There have been massive fines and forced consumer compensation payouts over illicit activity by these corporates. As a result, all the major banks have sold their financial planning operations. It has also seen a mass exodus of institutions and financial planners who did not want to step up to the professional standards that now exist for the profession. But under the regulations, full independence devoid of conflicts of interest is rare, and we treasure ours.

Chapter 14

People and professional standards

Hiring and firing are probably the two greatest challenges for management. Over my years in management positions, I learnt from bitter experience that the old business concept of 'hire slowly, fire quickly' is good business practice. Most managers, including me, think they are great judges of character when it comes to hiring people, but that is often not the case. I have had many experiences over the years where I have made poor employment decisions and paid a hefty price in some instances. Unfortunately, my experiences with headhunters and recruitment companies have been less than satisfactory.

One instance I recall was through a highly regarded international recruitment firm when I was looking to employ a secretary/receptionist. I interviewed a young lady who I thought was ideal for the role, and based on the recruitment company's report as to her experience and skills, I employed her. Within a couple of weeks, it was obvious that she had little or no experience, and what is more, she couldn't even type!

Our most costly appointment was when my son Andrew assumed the managing director role from me, and our long-time practice manager, Effie Goumas, had resigned to pursue an alternative career. We then decided to employ a general manager. We used a headhunter and, on his recommendation, we subsequently employed a fellow who presented well, said all the right things and had an impressive resume. Over the ensuing months, Andrew had continuing issues with this fellow, from discovering misrepresentation of key issues and project status reporting to inappropriate behaviour with staff communications. After several months, we had no option but to terminate him, and, in retrospect, we should have acted much earlier. We were to later discover that he had not been paying accounts and suppliers had been complaining. He had been hiding communications and blatantly lying about everything. Our staff were also extremely unhappy with his demeanour and certain matters concerning payroll.

This appointment had seriously hurt our relationships, and it took months to repair the damage. Fortunately, for us, Effie's career move hadn't worked out, and she agreed to return and clean up the mess.

We have had some other disappointments over the years, and I now appreciate the damage that bad hires can cause, not just in respect to their ability to do the job but the impact on the internal culture of the business. Luckily, these instances were rare.

I had a firm belief in the employment of good people with the potential to grow and the desire to reach their potential. I wanted to surround myself with people who wanted to share the mission to build something special and would provide them with an environment of excellence, fun and achievement. I wanted to create a workplace where people enjoyed working and achieved personal fulfilment, not just somewhere to earn a living.

This desire to employ and encourage great people applied to everyone in the organisation, not just the professional advisers. In my mind, everyone has a key role to play in achieving the desired result, with an organisation only being as strong as its weakest link. Everyone is special and a valuable part of the team. We offered everyone the opportunity to become involved in self-improvement, and we sponsored their further education. Empowerment of the individual was key to the development of a dynamic team of motivated and talented people, our internal culture and our overall flat management business structure.

I have a dislike for people who want to play the power game by treating others as being beneath them. I learnt early in my career in the office fit-out industry, where I dealt with both top executives and line managers, that those who really had the power did not need to prove it to anyone. I never ask people to do anything I would not do myself. I used to make a point of washing my own dishes, taking out the rubbish and performing menial tasks. If it was good enough for me, it was good enough for everyone else.

We gradually built a strong culture of belonging, mutual respect and commitment, which made for a fun day at the office and an elevated level of mutual respect.

From the get-go, I could see the potential for financial planning to become a truly recognised profession. Given my accounting experience, I saw the Australian Society of Accountants (now CPA Australia) progress from a diploma entry education standard to a bachelor's degree entry standard and the Certified Practicing Accountant postgraduate professional program. To me, it was only a matter of time that this evolutionary trend would also apply to financial planners.

I saw this as an exciting opportunity to build a business based on professional values with the potential to be recognised as a true and distinct profession. But it was not going to be easy, as in the early days financial planners typically operated on product-based commissions and had a poor reputation.

The Financial Planning Association of Australia (FPA) was established in 1992, and from then on, the financial planning profession began to evolve with the development of a diploma qualification and the introduction of the internationally recognised Certified Financial Planner (CFP) professional program in 1992.

One of my most vivid memories was attending the FPA Annual Convention in Canberra in 1992, where one of the plenary speakers was former New Zealand prime minister David Lange, who spoke about the requirements to become a recognised profession. It was a powerful address that excited me and motivated me to get involved.

I originally trained in accountancy but did not ever practice the profession; I merely worked in the accounting sections of companies and eventually changed direction. But I now felt motivated to pursue a career path that I knew would develop into a profession.

I became heavily involved in the development of the financial planning profession globally, to which I will refer in a further chapter.

In 1995, I developed our graduate mentoring program, which was our internal policy standard for professional practitioners. The policy consisted of recruiting commerce/business graduates and putting them through a mentoring program whilst they completed their postgraduate specialist training in financial planning. This would be a graduate diploma or master's degree – usually the latter. Then they would complete the CFP professional program. This was typically a 5-year progression, and in the meantime, they were learning the communication and relationship skills a professional adviser requires. They also learnt the company's philosophies, policies and business practices.

This is an expensive regime, however, as there is a lengthy lead time before graduates complete their specialist qualifications and eventually become business producers. Funding their development, their study courses and their attendance at conferences and training programs is costly, but retaining their patience, loyalty and enthusiasm is important. I saw it as an investment in the future and the best way to achieve our outcomes. I also saw it as a method to leverage my time and skills as they gradually took over my clients and eventually developed their own. That process has continued with subsequent advisers as we continue to grow. It has been an extremely successful and worthwhile initiative that has not only produced an outstanding group of professional advisers providing first class advice but has underpinned the development of our business succession plan.

Interestingly, around 2016 I was summoned to a meeting with the Deputy Commissioner of Australian Security & Investment Commission (ASIC), Peter Kell, after I wrote to the then ASIC Commissioner Greg Medcraft complaining about his outrageous comments in the press criticising the financial planning profession, who were a key component of his regulation portfolio. I had known Peter for years when he served on the ASIC board. Having discussed the issues surrounding Medcraft's press article, I was surprised at Peter's lack of intimate knowledge of what was happening in the real world with respect to standards and education. When I explained our graduate mentoring policy and processes, both he and his assistant were speechless. They looked at each other and asked me how we retained graduates through a program like that. Of course, the answer to that was attractive remuneration, belonging to a high-quality, successful organisation and the opportunity for future ownership.

When recruiting graduate appointees, I made it clear from the outset that their career path would lead to an opportunity for acquiring a share of business ownership, given that they had met their education and personal development requirements. This was important as it gave them an ultimate long-term goal and kept them motivated to develop over time. These were Gen X and Yers who wanted everything yesterday, so it was important to keep them engaged and motivated. We paid them well as they developed, and progressively increased their level of empowerment. Under our rules, they would not be appointed to act alone for clients until they had completed their education, but they were constantly engaged and communicating with clients under the mentorship of a senior adviser, in other words, learning the craft.

I should point out, the regulator's education requirement for licensed financial planners at that time was below diploma standard, so we were setting the bar extremely high. But I knew that eventually that is where the bar would be set. What I did not know was that it would take more than 20 years to get there.

The graduate mentoring regime continues to this day and has been responsible for developing a team of like-minded professional advisers who have taken the profession to another level of excellence and provided generational leadership of the business. I marvel at the quality of people we have attained and for their future.

I should add that whilst I had attained the CFP professional designation, I did not have a bachelor's degree. I figured I needed to walk the walk, not just talk the talk, and so I embarked on a master's degree in financial planning, which I completed in 2005 at the age of 58.

We have always aimed at being seen as an employer of choice. We focus on personal development and providing an outstanding working environment and attractive conditions. For example, from early on in the piece, we offered employees paid private health cover, income protection insurance and gym membership, and aimed to pay salaries above the industry standard.

I am proud of the fact that our business fosters long-term employees. We have had our failures along the way, but they are rare. We have a prominent level of long-term team members, many of whom have been with us for over 20 years.

Chapter 15

Empowerment and culture

I mentioned in the Preface, my business philosophy was heavily influenced by Robert Townsend's book *Up the Organisation*. This book attacked the traditional management structure consisting of layers of management, or as I like to call them, 'towers of power'.

I have a fanatical belief in empowerment and have seen firsthand how powerful it is in building a high-performance organisation like ours.

In the past, traditional structured management models consisted of layered tiers of management from the board to the managing director, descending throughout the organisation at tiered levels of responsibility. It was a 'bottom up' progression model, where those at the bottom aspired to climb the ladder of seniority. This fostered competition between the aspirants, and typically a 'claim and blame' environment resulted where managers fought to protect their position with their superiors whilst they vied for promotion. I had experienced this type of structure through my corporate life and found it ineffective, inefficient, structurally flawed and saturated with conflicts of self-interest.

Managers would typically 'claim' credit for any positive performance outcomes by their team and be quick to lay the 'blame' for deficient performance on someone else. This resulted in a culture of mistrust and a reluctance for anyone to step up for fear their ideas would be claimed by their manager. Climbing the corporate ladder was a bit of a self-interest blood sport and hardly conducive to excellent quality dynamic management.

These people were typically very protective of their position on the management ladder, which flows through to their decision-making. For example, in the process of hiring staff, they would look for someone competent but not so competent that they may become a threat. This results in a mediocre workforce with no initiative or development potential.

There is a splendid example of the problems with tiered management in the movie *Ford v Ferrari*, where corporate interference almost stalled Ford's challenge of Ferrari in the Le Mans 24-hour race. The manager in charge of the Ford project was sceptical and had a healthy disrespect for the car designer Carroll Shelby and his race driver Ken Miles, who were leading the development team. He constantly put up barricades and kept Henry Ford in the dark. It was only when Shelby, being completely disillusioned, went behind the corporate manager's back and acquainted Henry Ford with the facts that the challenge took place, and Ford was eventually triumphant.

Ford Motor company executives, led by Henry Ford Jnr. had decided to use the Le Mans race as a method to enhance its image as an innovative car producer by defeating the all-conquering Ferrari team.

Henry Ford met with Carroll Shelby who convinced him that he was the only person who could help Ford win as he was the only American to win the Le Mans race along with his driver Ken Miles. Ford agreed and appointed him to lead the project.

Ford executives were outraged that they had been usurped and successfully conspired to bring Shelby and Miles down.

When the executive team's version of the Shelby car finally raced they were uncompetitive and Shelby confronted Ford to convince hin he had made a mistake in sacking him and Miles. Ford reappointed Shelby and Miles who subsequently won the race over the Ferrari team.

This was a clear exemple of executive ego and seld-importance regardless of a compromised outcome. Under the empowerment model, the ecxeutive team would have embraced the proven skills of Shelby amd Miles for the collective success of the mission.

Empowerment is achieved when ownership of the task is assigned to the individual, that is, you encourage team members to take control and assume total responsibility for their role without the need for constant supervision. It is also about using personal initiatives to develop the role, solve problems and achieve positive outcomes. This creates an atmosphere of excitement and dedication to the achievement of success, with everyone empowered to work together.

Hiring quality people is vital in developing a team of self-dependent individuals taking individual responsibility for their roles and who support each other in achieving a common goal of service delivery. When I say 'quality' people, it is not just about academic ability, it is very much about character and personal attributes as well.

Empowerment also comes from the top and involves sharing the dream, the mission, the passion, core beliefs and standards. It entails mutual trust and respect, encourages initiative, then recognises, celebrates and rewards positive outcomes. It certainly shares ownership and responsibility for the task, but it is not abandonment. It requires continuous mentoring, support and comradeship as needed.

A democratic management style is essential. Autocratic leaders are dictatorial in nature, which is about control and not conducive to the empowerment of others. I am by nature a democratic leader and always have been collaborative. In my corporate experience, I used empowerment techniques in my teams, which were phenomenally successful even within a traditional tiered management regime.

I first employed empowerment strategies with the establishment of the Brisbane branch of Brash's wholesale business (AMI). I had a staff of seven and impressed upon them the importance of taking ownership of their task and using their initiative. We had a successful and vibrant business with everyone taking responsibility for their own task but also working as a cohesive team. Every Friday at 4 pm we had our weekly team meeting, and I would ask them all to recognise one of their peers for a special effort during the past week. This engendered a spirit of recognition, celebration and reward within the team.

An example of the success of empowerment theory was when I hired a young storeman by the name of George. He was aged in his early 20s, married with a young child. He had left school early and had not done much to progress himself but now realised that he had responsibilities and had to step up. He was a nice young man, and I admired his attitude, so I employed him. I then went about empowering George to become responsible for our warehouse, including scheduling container shipments from the wharves and dispatching goods throughout Queensland.

George was sensational. He grew so much in his ability to take charge of his responsibilities, and his personal development was off the chart. George would attend our weekly meetings in the office and get himself all dressed up for the occasion. Everyone loved him, and he was an absolute model of the empowerment philosophy. It was life-changing for both George and his family, and we had a first-class warehouse manager.

Eventually, George landed a better job with more prospects with another company, and I was delighted for him. We could not offer him similar future growth opportunities, so I accepted he had to leave. I have a firm belief that regardless of the development you put into good people, you must accept that if you cannot offer them future growth opportunities, they will leave. I still count that as a win and accept it as a fact of life.

Empowerment is about nurturing, mentoring, and then challenging good people to take responsibility, use their initiative and make their own decisions. By sharing the passion and the dream, empowerment results in buy-in by the team, and so they adopt the passion, and it creates an atmosphere of genuine joy and enthusiasm in the joint ownership of something special. But the real secret is mutual trust and the ability of the founder to genuinely expose their passion and core beliefs and share ownership of the mission.

Delegation is often confused with empowerment but is an entirely different thing. Delegation means assigning a task but not the ownership nor the responsibility for outcomes. The delegator retains responsibility and control over the task and takes credit for the outcome. Empowerment means transferring the entire ownership, responsibility, accountability and decision-making of a role. It also means transferring the kudos and reward that go with the success of the task.

We often reinforce to our team that we do not want to hear about problems and errors, we understand they are going to happen. What we want to be told is how they fixed problems and turned them into benefits. We deal with people's money, and it is a serious business with all sorts of regulatory responsibilities. We take these matters seriously, and we need to know when things go wrong. But we also need our people to know that we are not into playing the 'blame game' and want them to take ownership of rectifying and reporting. This returns a number of benefits. Our team knows that we trust them to recognise errors, giving them the power to rectify them and then the comfort of recording the resolution. Importantly, where an error involves a client, individuals are empowered to notify the clients, tell them how it has been resolved and offer some form of gift of appreciation. The usual result is that the client is thrilled at the outcome, thankful for the attention, the team member gets the kudos, and compliance is fulfilled. Turning the lemon into lemonade – win, win, win!

I am not suggesting that we were comfortable accepting mistakes. I accept that people will make mistakes, learn and move on. But repetition of mistakes is carelessness and needs to be counselled.

I always made it clear to my colleagues that I hired them because they were smarter than me and would make me redundant one day. And they did.

The worst mistake made by businesses is that the founder, the entrepreneur, if you like, always thinks the business depends on them and that no-one can do it better than they can. That may be true, but a business that depends on a keyperson is structurally weak, subject to elevated risk of something happening to the keyperson and limited in its growth and value potential. Moreover, its growth is dependent on employing other professionals who, without equity participation or incentive lock-in, are likely to be poached or simply start up on their own. Throughout my succession speaking experience, the common complaint by business owners was their inability to hold quality people, so that when they were planning to exit, they had no-one internally who could take over the business or provide sustainability.

In my experience, planning for a business exit needs at least 10 years to develop talent and establish the process. I will expand on this more under the discussion on corporatisation and succession.

Empowerment is not easy. It requires tolerance and understanding. There will be times when colleagues do not do things exactly as you would, but if they achieve the desired result, it is about acceptance of the differences and continuing to counsel and encourage. For instance, 'Hey Sue, that was a great outcome you achieved, and I really loved the way you went about it. Just as a thought, you might also consider ...'. Recognise, reward and counsel.

I have many success stories I could share, but one is about my first appointee, Janine. She grew from a competent secretary/personal assistant to become an extraordinary contributor to the creation of our innovative systems and dedicated to owning the mission. She developed her skills and became a highly paid operations manager, systems designer and IT developer. As a result of her role in our systems development and her commitment and loyalty, we gave her 5% of the business.

Another somewhat amusing story is the appointment of my long-term Executive Assistant (EA), Clare. It was during my time as Chairman of the Financial Planning Association (FPA), which often required me to be absent from the office. We were advertising for an executive assistant following the resignation of my former PA/receptionist following childbirth.

On the day I had an appointment with Clare, who was a candidate for the EA role, I was held up at a meeting at the FPA office. I kept calling to tell Janine that I was on my way, and could she look after Clare until I arrived. When I finally arrived at the office, I could hear much laughter emanating from the boardroom. As I opened the door, Janine introduced Clare and announced that she was a perfect fit for the job, and she had already hired her. I stood there speechless and then attempted to lamely ask Clare some questions, which was clearly a waste of time. As it transpired, Clare was a sensational choice and became a valuable asset to the business for over 20 years. Talk about being made redundant!

The team retreat

One of the best empowerment and strategic planning decisions I ever made was the creation of our team retreats.

In 1994, following the Wilson saga and the commencement of our new beginning, I had the thought that it would be great to take the entire team away together and spend a couple of days workshopping the business and just bonding as a team.

In the first year, we shut down the office over a Thursday afternoon and Friday and took our team of five people to Mount Eliza business school for a think tank through to Saturday. We did this twice annually for a few years but then reduced to once a year as our numbers grew and the agenda and preparation became more complex. We always worked extremely hard and found it difficult to stop at the end of the day. But we also had a huge amount of fun together playing wacky games, arranging themed dinners, singing karaoke or just having fun. It was an extraordinary and unique experience and built a bond and a level of camaraderie that was beyond any expectation I might have had.

The retreat rules are simple:

- Leave your egos at the door; everyone is equal and their opinion valuable.

- No idea is a bad idea. If a thought comes to mind, put it out on the table.

- No secrets – share all the facts about the business with everyone.

- Whatever decisions are made by the group will be implemented by the business within 90 day**s**.

Now this last rule was the key. It is pointless asking people to give their opinions and ideas if the company does not implement them.

Our team numbers have grown to more than 60. But it remains the most powerful and creative strategic activity we do. I am continually surprised at the power of these getaways. The creative ideas on everything from systems design and innovation to enhanced client services, improved procedures and even office design. It never ceases to amaze me.

We usually started the retreat agenda with a whip around the table for attendees to talk about something personal to them. For example, something they were proud of achieving or a challenge they had overcome. The raw emotion and willingness to share their innermost feelings were alarming and so powerful. There were tears and hugs, and that close feeling of mutual trust permeated through the entire time at the retreat and beyond.

Apart from the specific outcomes, which were amazing in themselves, was the sharing of ownership of the decisions. Here we were making key business decisions for which the entire group had ownership and buy-in. As a result, we all shared in celebrating the outcomes.

As an example, at one of our retreats, the issue of our office accommodation came up for discussion. The group came to the decision that we needed more space and had to move offices. After the lunch break, I came back into the meeting room to find the group searching realestate.com.au for new business premises. We specified the search area, and I empowered my EA Clare and our Practice Manager: Effie to take charge of finding prospective offices. Within two months, we had signed a lease and commenced the fit-out design.

The retreats themselves were exhilarating and creative, but the ideas that came from all members of our team were just unbelievable at times. The outcomes were always extraordinary and incredibly innovative. These were the 'aha' moments.

As I said, we closed the office for two days, which might seem crazy. But we forewarned the clients and monitored the telephones throughout so we could respond to any urgent matters. But a side benefit was that we shared all this with our clients. They knew what we were doing and could not wait to hear what we discussed and the outcomes we reached. In a way, we were empowering our clients by including them in the process.

Nothing is perfect

I am passionate about empowerment and thankful for what it has meant to us over the years. But like everything, it can have its problems.

On the positive side, empowerment tends to create long-term employees. This can become an issue, however, in a growing business where change is inevitable and can result in resistance to change for those who cannot cope with that change.

Personally, I am a change freak. I love change and thrive on it. But sometimes, others cannot cope with a change to their comfort zone within an organisation and resist it. This can manifest in an empowered person making decisions and taking actions that suit their past experiences and refusing to adapt to changes.

One such person was Janine. She had a powerful position within the company, as a result of her embracing the concept of empowerment, but she then resented the influx of new, younger professionals who she saw as a threat to her position and put her out of her comfort zone. Unfortunately, the tensions that resulted became intolerable, and in preparation for my handing over the leadership role, I needed to resolve the situation. In the end, I had to make her an attractive offer to retire when I was handing over the management to my younger colleagues. I knew there would be a destructive confrontation if I did not act, but likewise, I wanted to be sure she was looked after following 30 years of loyal service.

Another issue is the 'Peter principle', where people are promoted beyond their capability. This happened a couple of times and caused us to lose good people. This was sad, and I regret my poor judgement at the time.

As time goes on and the business grows bigger, these issues tend to go away. In fact, the culture tends to take care of them. Anyone who refuses to live the culture and share the mission will find it difficult to survive in this environment. Not by virtue of any nastiness or pressure, it just is what it is, and trying to swim against the tide is impossible.

My experience and the outcomes we achieved prove conclusively that the empowerment model builds dynamic and high-powered organisations. It generates an energy and team-focused force that is driven to success through the pursuit of excellence and a commitment to a common mission. It is also key to building a business to last indefinitely.

The office

In 1987, we started out in a small office in St Kilda Road, Melbourne, then swapped to a larger office suite with a neighbouring law firm in 1990. Then, in 1996, I purchased a small office building in suburban South Yarra, which was a redeveloped terrace house that we loved. Having outgrown this office, in 2001, we sold and purchased a strata-titled office in a building in Caulfield.

I mentioned earlier that our next office move, in 2006, was determined by the team at a staff retreat, but, unfortunately, we could not find a suitable office to purchase, so we reverted to renting. This office was in South Melbourne, closer to the Melbourne CBD. With all these premises, I always involved my team in the selection and design of the offices and the fit-outs.

We moved to our current offices in 2016 and then expanded to take on the entire 8th floor in 2020. My son, Andrew, had assumed the role as Managing Director, and he included the subject of office design on the agenda of a subsequent team retreat. The object was to break into breakout groups and brainstorm ideas that the group would like to be incorporated into the office environment. Sensational ideas came forth and formed the basis for the ultimate outcome.

In briefing the designers, Andrew involved the input of team members and consulted along the way. He used the retreat ideas to provide the designers with the functionality we desired, which was based on fun, free communication and a relaxed, friendly and welcoming atmosphere. Of course, we are a professional organisation, so it also had to be appropriate.

Once the layout design was agreed, Andrew empowered members of the team to determine the final changes, like furniture choices and colours.

The office is a revelation. The entrance is professional but quickly takes on an atmosphere of homeliness and style. The feeling you get when you enter is magical. When clients visit this area, it often turns into a family gathering between the clients and their team of contacts. Our 'front of office', Leonnie, is an absolute gem and makes the client experience something special.

The central office is open plan, spacious, light and airy. It features greenery and generous workstations with open space. There are offices for those who need the privacy, but many discussions and group meetings are held in other areas that are less formal. The staff amenities area is exceptionally large, consisting of a full kitchen, tables and chairs of assorted sizes, and booths where groups can gather for more relaxed meetings. There is a table tennis table and a big screen TV, so the room can be used for multiple purposes. It is not unusual to see clients sitting in this area with their advisers, as they love to get involved with everyone.

Our meeting rooms are themed sitting rooms, such as 'The Library', which are comfortable and relaxed. We also have a formal boardroom, a large meeting/training room and other rooms with audiovisual capability, when required.

The overriding atmosphere of the office space reflects our culture. It is infectious and unmistakeable. It is a joy to go there, and of course it is enhanced by the people that work in an atmosphere of enthusiasm, commitment and camaraderie.

A by-product of empowerment is the development of culture. Culture is defined as 'a shared asset of values and beliefs'. A great business culture runs much deeper than that, however, and that is the hard stuff that most businesses do not understand.

A great culture starts at the top and is about sharing the passion, belief, ownership of the mission and commitment to one another. It is an atmosphere of joy, enthusiasm, camaraderie, respect and compassion. These are all emotive words that are rarely spoken in a boardroom, but for us it was a daily reality. Empowerment built a culture that was quite extraordinary. I get goosebumps every time I think about it. It is so electric and contagious it just drives success on every level, but most importantly, in client satisfaction and a sense of belonging.

The starting point for building a great culture is for the founder to be open to sharing the passion, the dream and the mission. This is not easy for people to do because it means exposing your innermost feelings and ideals. It can and should be emotionally charged. Others cannot be expected to be inspired to share the journey if the message is not emotionally charged, and they will respond to the trust of sharing with them.

Culture consists of a shared set of values, passions and standards by like-minded people with an elevated level of mutual respect. They need to jointly own the mission and be empowered to play their part in achieving mutually shared success. All these elements initially come from the top and progressively permeate and become the culture of the organisation. Leading by example is an imperative element for everyone to embrace.

To quote the movie *Field of Dreams* – 'If you build it, they will come'. That sums up my belief in the development of good culture. If a business has a high-level set of standards and principles to which it is passionately committed and shares that with its people, they will embrace and share the passion. Quality and standards are things to which everyone is attracted, particularly quality people and high achievers.

We constantly get feedback from people who visit our office that they can feel our culture in the air as soon as you enter the reception area. It is unmistakable and infectious. For example, we invite an external provider to run a 360 review of our business every couple of years. This involves every team member completing a questionnaire about their peers, direct reports and the business, followed by an interview with a specialist to review the results. The regular comment from these external consultants is that our culture is almost unbelievable. One even asked if they could have a job with us!

Building a great culture takes work and commitment, but once achieved, it cannot be ignored. Culture is a living thing and must become part of an organisation's DNA on a daily basis. If not, it will die.

Chapter 16

Corporatisation and intrinsic value

Corporatisation

The primary challenge for any business is to survive the early establishment phase and then develop infrastructure and viability. It is then important to move out of the 'key person' stage where the business is solely reliant on one person to become a business in the true sense of the word. This is what I call 'corporatisation'.

Corporatisation occurs when the business either hires staff who have the capacity to drive the business in the absence of the key person and could, if something were to happen to the key person, continue to operate.

Under our empowerment model, we hired highly competent people and then trained, nurtured and empowered them to take leadership responsibility in their roles. This ensured that the business very quickly and effectively became less dependent on the key person and eventually became self-dependent.

Developments of systems, processes and infrastructure are also a vital element of corporatisation. As I will relate later, this was a key issue for us and an opportunity for developing innovative state-of-the-art systems and retaining control of data so that we were entirely self-sufficient in this regard. This is a critical stage in the evolution and life cycle of any business going forward.

As we developed our financial planning colleagues through our mentoring program, we prepared them to take control of our client base. One of the challenges of a professional advice and service business is that the clients tend to deal with individual advisers and form close relationships. Whilst this is obviously desirable, it can pose a major threat to the business as advisers may choose to leave and the clients follow them, or internal transitioning of clients within the business to manage growth pressures or retirements can be difficult. Likewise, it is important to create an environment where clients are provided with immediate attention in the event their primary adviser is unavailable.

As part of our graduate mentoring program and our internal client service model, I developed a multi-point contact approach where clients would have a primary advice contact but also an internal account administrator and secondary advice contact with an associate adviser. We also maintained constant communication between the business and the client base. The outcome of this was to ensure that the clients had a close relationship with our internal community as well as their primary reports and were therefore a part of our 'family'.

As I pointed out earlier in my experience with changing licensees, the client will determine their own loyalties, and it is therefore important for them to have multiple relationships within the business. Whilst we always have restraint clauses in our employment contracts, it is the client's relationship that dictates loyalty and retention.

Another important aspect of corporatisation is to facilitate the transfer of clients to alternative advisers and to have all staff equipped and able to provide service to all clients. If advisers are incentivised purely by individual business production, they will be reluctant to service other adviser's clients or perform other duties that are not related to their own business production.

We consider all clients as clients of the business, and all clients have multiple personal contacts within the firm and ongoing relationships with the business. That is not to say they did not have strong personal connections with individuals, they did.

A large part of our corporatisation plan was the ability to transition clients from one adviser to another. It is a product of growth that advisers will continue to grow their client base to a point where they have no capacity. In my case, I had built a large client base, but my management responsibilities had grown so that I had surpassed capacity. I had no ability to take on new clients and needed other advisers to service my referral network.

This is another big problem for growing businesses. You do not want your key business drivers to become administrators. But it is inevitable for growing businesses to multitask key people until the business can afford to employ full-time specialists to key positions. This is a critical time in any business evolution.

As we appointed graduates, they were assigned to a senior adviser, who worked side by side with them in contacting clients and attending meetings. By the time they had completed their mentorship, they had all the skills they needed, including client interfacing, to seamlessly transition and take control of a client's affairs. This worked beautifully, and the clients had no issue with it. They could still contact their original adviser, if necessary, but that was rare.

Eventually, we had successfully achieved corporatisation and I had successfully made myself redundant.

Intrinsic value

Financial planning can often be a transaction-based business. That is, an adviser can advise a client on their investments, place the investments and send the client on their way to fend for themselves. There was little or no continuity of the relationship and no continuity of revenue, but more importantly, a poor outcome for the clients. So, the business had to renew itself every day and had little intrinsic or market value. I could see this was a bad business model where you had to reinvent the business every day and build no intrinsic value at all. But moreover, this was completely inadequate and inappropriate for the client.

Intrinsic value is the net value of assets and recurrent revenue; that is, revenue that is subject to an ongoing agreement with permanent clients and effectively guaranteed.

From a business point of view, I was determined to develop a business with recurrent relation-based revenue and, thus, one with an ongoing reliable revenue stream that would provide financial security and intrinsic value. But clearly, such a relationship needed to be justified and represent true value to the client.

I commented earlier that the business plan should not be revenue-driven, but it was a crucial element in developing a good business. Intrinsic value and a recurrent revenue stream were certainly a sound business-based element, but they were aligned with a service model that was based on quality service delivery, client best interests and achieving client outcomes.

Financial planning is complex and certainly not 'set and forget'. It requires an ongoing relationship and professional management. Clients had no idea how to manage their investments, and to just put their money into managed investments and send them on their way was almost criminal neglect.

People's circumstances continually change as they go through phases of their lives, so whilst an initial financial plan may be relevant, long-term changes in circumstances need to be considered along the way and changes made to the master plan. Therefore, there was an absolute need for an ongoing close relationship between the client and their financial planner.

Because of our fee-based model, we were able to strike fair and competitive pricing with an emphasis on the long-term relationship. We did not charge an initial asset fee, and where we saw a need to invest in managed products, we either used wholesale funds whose charges were not inflated by commissions or we rebated commissions to the client. We charged for our work in developing initial advice, but our ongoing fee was all-inclusive of future advice and portfolio administration. Because of our system's efficiency, we were able to hand these savings back to the clients in the form of reduced fees. We estimate that our overall annual charging rate was around half the industry average.

The combination of high-level service offerings for lower costs defies the norm, but it is a powerful offering.

Our revenue is around 95% recurrent, that is, consisting of ongoing annual client fees. It makes for a financially viable and secure business model and translates into a strong intrinsic value.

Chapter 17

Business evolution: designing the succession plan

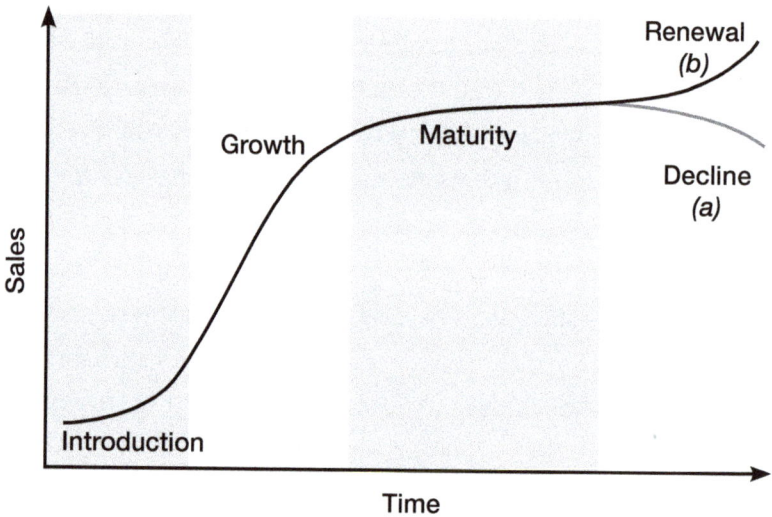

All businesses go through a similar evolutionary process. In most cases, businesses start as a 'key person' start-up and are often undercapitalised. As businesses progress through their various stages of development, the trends are typical.

History shows that 60% of small business start-ups fail in the first three years, and overall, 90% will fail. Most fail due to undercapitalisation and no sound business planning, amongst other things. I was aware of that from my experience, so I was careful to develop a logical and feasible business plan to put in place and then develop the market accordingly.

Introduction: the start up

This is the establishment phase and the most dangerous time for any business. Typically, it is about making sales and developing a cash flow to keep the business operational and is the phase where most start-up businesses fail. This flows into the growth phase, which entails hiring staff, developing systems, processes and infrastructure. To this point, businesses are prone to fail due to a lack of market penetration or a shortage of capital.

Growth phase

During the growth phase, the business is established but profits are thin, so growth is essential. This stage is about developing networks, leveraging business development and aiming to corporatise. It is during this phase that the business is at its peak dynamic performance, driving growth and having the financial ability to develop to fund operational development.

Maturity

When the business reaches the maturity stage, it has established reliable markets, solid revenue streams and good profitability. It tends to relax intensity and become comfortable. When most companies get to this stage, there is a propensity to take the foot off the accelerator and 'consolidate'. The 'if it ain't broke, don't fix it' attitude tends to come into play, and the business can fall into complacency.

This is the most dangerous time for most companies. Complacency sets in, and if not addressed, the business will decline. I see examples of this all the time with business owners who are reluctant to get out of their comfort zone and keep pace with change.

Renewal

Renewal is the important part of business evolution that is difficult for many companies to come to grips with. In a business that began with a key person founder, facing the prospect of a radical change in leadership and the injection of new vitality can be a challenge. In my case, it had been baked in from the start and made perfect sense to me. I do not suggest that I did not have anxious moments, but I was happy to pass over the reins and support the transition.

There are examples of big, successful corporations that were market leaders in their field but failed to adapt to change with catastrophic results. One that comes to mind is Kodak, which had a massive market share of the global photography equipment, film and accessory business. Although it had researched digital photography back in the 1980s, management complacency failed to act quickly enough in developing and marketing the innovative technology. Very quickly it was overrun and finally went bankrupt in 2012, (emerging from bankruptcy in 2013). Three other examples include Nokia, who dominated the mobile phone market before Apple, with Microsoft acquiring Nokia's mobile phone business in 2014 due to poor management decisions; Sony, whose Walkman (1979 to 2010) had hold of·the portable music market did not adapt to change before the Apple iPod took over; and Encyclopaedia Britannica, whose move into digital technology took place in a very competitive market, suffered financial difficulties in the face of change.

Renewal includes new thinking, embracing change and adapting to new developments. Complacency is the enemy. There needs to be preparation and forward planning well prior to this time so the business is geared up to enter the renewal phase and re-energise before the decline or complacency occurs. Succession was a core belief of mine, and I was totally committed to the renewal phase of the business upon it reaching the maturity stage and its longevity.

My succession plan was designed to deal with this evolutionary cycle, but the trick is for the founder to recognise when it is time to act and be willing to hand over the reins. Obviously, this is a massive problem for most businesspeople to deal with, but my focus was very much placed on the best interests of the business and its stakeholders, particularly the clients and the staff..

In our case, succession included a change in business ownership. Obviously, young people do not have access to funds or equity to secure funding for a business purchase. This was a hurdle we had to overcome, and I knew the retail banks would not entertain us. I had a close relationship with Dean Firth[1], our business manager at Macquarie Bank, who were now also our business bankers. Dean and I would meet regularly for breakfast and talk about all sorts of stuff. I raised with him the opportunity for funding equity acquisitions in financial planning practices. We talked about it and gradually formulated a prospective model. Dean went away and put a proposal to the bank's management, and it was decided to develop a formal proposal using our practice as a case study. From that came Macquarie's equity funding facility, which helped us to develop an equity sharing model.

Our model is that we arrange for the lending from Macquarie, which is a personal loan to the purchaser, but we secure the loan against the value of the company. The dividends generated by their equity profit share repay the loan over a few years, and then they benefit personally from the profit generation. Over

---

1   Dean Firth is now Head of Business Banking at Macquarie Bank.

time under this model, issues of business success, value and income become the major focus.

It could be argued that I had sacrificed a great deal by progressively selling the company, which is now unbelievably valuable. But I do not see it that way. In the first instance, business owners have an entirely different mindset from employees, and I needed that element to drive the business forward. Secondly, there is no way I could have built the business into what it has become without my partners' commitment and our empowerment model. As I tell my partners, this is effectively gearing your personal capacity and the growth potential of the business.

As my associates reached the latter part of their training, I began to introduce them to my referral network, and over time they built trusting relationships and took over the network to build their client base within the company.

Overall, we had a progressive and smooth transition of the existing client base and the future inflow of new business. Over time, my younger colleagues also looked to broaden their own referral networks for the benefit of the business.

In 2015, I had five partners, all of whom were of excellent character but none who had any management experience other than their empowerment experience within the company. In collaboration with our chair, Rob Roberts, we concluded that we should preferably make an internal appointment due to the relative simplicity of the business and the nature of the flat structure we had created.

To explain further, our business consists of winning new clients and providing exemplary service to ensure client loyalty and longevity. Obviously, there are systemic complexities, but that is what we did. My partners were all senior advisers and were the key drivers of the business, so there was no justification for adding another layer of management over the top.

The problem I had was that one of my partners was my son Andrew, so I clearly had to step away from the evaluation of candidates. Rob and an external psychologist with expertise in the field took over the role of evaluating and recommending my successor, although I was to be involved in the final decision. The three most senior partners, including Andrew, expressed interest in the managing director role.

Following a lengthy series of interviews, a psychological assessment and analysis, one of the candidates withdrew, and as it happened, Andrew was seen as clearly the preferred candidate and subsequently appointed. Whilst Andrew was evaluated by others and deserved his appointment, there had to be feelings of nepotism amongst his peers, but I could not let myself be concerned with this. Andrew was duly appointed and adopts an inclusive management style with his senior colleagues that seems to work well.

I explained earlier that I am addicted to change and innovation, and this was just another example of that. The business was in great shape and was a dynamic operation, but it would need new energy, innovative ideas and renewed enthusiasm to prosper in the future. From where I sat, I had ticked off all my original hopes, dreams and core beliefs. I was still energetic and enthusiastic about the business but completely satisfied and happy to enter the next phase. As it happened, Rob Roberts had decided to retire at the same time, so I would assume the role of chair but separate from the operational side of the business.

There is no question in my mind that this was the best decision for the business. The change brought about renewed energy, the latest ideas and innovation and a recharging of enthusiasm but retained the core beliefs and philosophies of the business. In addition, it ensured that the business leadership remained young and energetic. Our business is 40 years old, but the average age of its employees is around 35 years. Our shareholders, who comprise our leadership team, range from early 30s to mid-40s and our associates are in their 20s and 30s. So, whilst our personnel are well experienced, it will remain youthful and vibrant under this regime.

Our graduate mentoring worked out to be an enormous success, and, apart from developing excellent professional advisers steeped in the company's philosophies and standards, I had opportunities to judge their character and determine whether they would make good equity partners.

Currently, my partners intend to continue the succession model, but that is out of my hands now, and I accept that what will be will be. I have no regrets and do not look backward. I am totally delighted with the outcomes and the prospects for the future.

Chapter 18

Succession: the implementation

From the outset, ownership succession was a key objective of mine. I wanted to create an organisation that was special and worthy of succeeding me into the future. I also wanted to create an environment of shared ownership, both emotionally and financially. This seemed to me to be a natural by-product of the empowerment model.

This really shaped my attitude towards hiring good people who had the character to grow and take the business forward. People who had the desire to succeed and reach their potential and eventually run the business.

I admit that my disastrous partnership experience solidified my commitment to my 'growth from within' policy. It also provided me with the opportunity to share my experience and knowledge and develop the buy-in and belief of the company's philosophies. In other words, ensuring the longevity of the business model and the service offering.

Succession takes years to develop, and along the way, effort is required to shape and develop people. It also impacted the way in which I communicated with my team and ensured that they shared the journey and understood the long-term plan for the business. This, in turn, gave them confidence in their long-term job security.

In my experience, my colleagues in small to medium businesses simply built their businesses with a view to eventually selling out to the highest bidder. I call it the 'selling the farm' model. A few had a profit-sharing model, but the vast majority did not share equity. There are issues with this, as businesses tend to remain as key person businesses with inherent risks and issues.

The biggest problem with the 'selling the farm' model is that it is difficult to retain good people without giving them an opportunity to participate in ownership. This is true of any professional advice business, as once practitioners learn their craft and can attract clients, they are often poached by another business or simply leave and develop their own business. Over the years, I have delivered numerous presentations on succession planning, and this issue of retaining talent was the most frequent problem with business owners.

Most business owners are loath to sell down the equity in their business because they want to retain it for themselves. My view is that progressively selling down equity significantly strengthens the growth potential of the business so that, eventually, the original owner's value of a reduced equity share is enhanced. I had no doubt that my equity would grow much greater in value than I could achieve alone. Likewise, my equity partners' share value will be leveraged over time. That is a win-win proposition for all concerned. Then there is the added sustainability of the business into the future, which was also important to me.

As noted earlier, a business that is reliant on a key person is high risk due to its dependence on one person; it is structurally weak and is limited in scope to achieve its growth potential. Good businesses aim to corporatise and develop a strong infrastructure of personnel, systems and processes. A strong succession plan is a vital cog in this process, in my opinion.

As I was building our business in the early years, one of the most frequent questions prospective clients would ask me was, 'What happens to us if something happens to you?' It was a tricky question to answer until I had appointed my first graduate, after which I could readily explain our succession plan, and this gave comfort to the clients.

The other issues that were particularly important to me were being able to provide longevity and continuity of the business to our clients. We developed a multi-generational business where we often looked after three generations of the same family, so longevity was important. My feeling was that we had a moral obligation to fulfil our promise of lifetime commitment to our clients.

Having developed my graduate mentoring policy in 1994, I employed my first associate, Chris Morcom, in 1997. Chris had worked in one of the large banks whilst studying his postgraduate accounting professional course with CPA Australia (Certified Practising Accountants of Australia). He then left the bank and worked part time to concentrate on his studies. Within the CPA program, he studied financial planning and developed a keen interest. He was recommended to me by a mutual friend, and at the end of our first meeting, Chris impressed me so much, as a person and by his attitude, that I offered him the position on the spot, which he accepted.

Chris and I quickly developed a great relationship, as he did with our team. But there was resistance from a couple of people to the introduction of a new element to the business that was likely to develop into a threat to their status. That was an interesting development to me, but it soon dissipated. We were still a small business with just six people, so it was a crucial step for us as it represented the start of my 'redundancy' plan to succession. It was my job to share the vision and make sure everyone was on the same page.

The first thing I had to overcome, with Chris and all our subsequent graduate appointments, was teaching them how to write business letters and reports. They came from a land at university where 'more is better' and they tended to write voluminously in unnatural language. I constantly went through their advice documents, crossing out large chunks of repetition or irrelevant information, asking them, 'Do you really think you speak like that?'

From 1997 to 2001, I was a director and then chair of the Financial Planning Association of Australia (FPA), a representative on the International Certified Financial Planners (CFP) Council, and then director of the Financial Planning Standards Board (FBSB), which meant I was away from the office a fair bit. One day I came into the office, and two of my long-term clients were waiting in reception. I was surprised to see them and asked if we had an appointment. They replied, 'No, we are here to see Chris.' At first, I was taken aback, but then I thought, 'How good this is!' The start of our smooth transition.

In 2003, we sold 10% of the business to Chris. Then, as each of our associate advisers completed their education and their personal development, they were promoted to senior client advisers and then offered the opportunity to acquire equity in the business. Since then, we have sold down a total of 95% equity amongst seven partners.

Our next graduate appointment failed to make the grade after being with us for a year or so, which was my first and only failure. In around 2000, I looked to employ another graduate and was most keen to find a female prospect, which was not easy as there were few available. I finally found a suitable candidate and appointed her. Having accepted our position, on the Thursday before the Monday she was meant to start, she called me and said she had an offer from another much larger company and could not decide. I made the decision for her and moved on. We then readvertised and appointed Glenn Fairbairn, who was working in the industry whilst completing his commerce/financial planning degree. I was disappointed to not appoint a female, but Glenn was an excellent choice and is now a senior equity partner.

At around the same time as we appointed Glenn, my son Andrew, who had completed a business/sports management degree, approached his mother and I to say that he had decided he would like to join the firm as he had lost interest in pursuing sports management. We were caught by surprise but were obviously delighted. Andrew is now managing director of the company.

Since then, we have appointed numerous graduates, and at the time of writing, 11 have become senior wealth advisers, and the company has eight equity owners. In addition, there are four senior associates and five associates going through the mentoring process, so our future is well secured.

This entire succession plan has been resoundingly successful, as these people are incredibly bright and enthusiastic. At the same time, they are mentored to embrace the business's ethical and practicing standards, our commitment to a client-first attitude and service delivery, and empowered to take ownership and responsibility for their role. Importantly, they learn the craft of advising and relationships, which are the people skills that are so important in our profession. Having the prospect of equity ownership engenders two-way commitment and a purpose for them to aim for and retain their interest through the process.

I am extremely pleased and proud of the successful ownership and leadership transition of our business, and the outcome speaks for itself. We have a business with the maturity of 40 years but a youthful, motivated, enthusiastic ownership and senior advice team with an average age of around 40 years.

We have continuity of the original philosophies, standards and core beliefs of the business through the transition and succession phase of like-minded people who have been brought up through the business in a structured growth path.

The business has a revenue that is 95% recurrent, so it is extraordinarily financially secure with a solid and consistent growth history.

From where I sit, I have achieved everything I wanted to achieve throughout this process and could not be more delighted with the outcome. I am happy for the success my colleagues will continue to achieve and to see our wonderful business and its relationships continue beyond me.

PART 3

Achieving outcomes

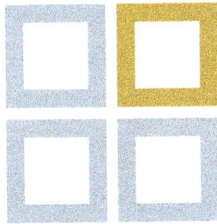

Chapter 19

The profession

My story has been about our journey and the beliefs and standards that drove me and my partners and teammates along the way. But, at the end of the day, it is all about achieving great outcomes in every sphere of influence, both internal and external.

In this part of my story, I have tried to encapsulate the outcomes we achieved as a result of the standards we set ourselves and attempted to influence our profession at large into achieving the ultimate goal of professionalism.

Ultimately, the outcomes that we achieved at the transition of my journey and beyond are the culmination of this story.

My involvement in the profession

I am a great believer that if you are not prepared to roll up your sleeves, contribute and get involved in the process, you haven't got the right to criticise and complain about the outcome.

During the 1980s, the Financial Planning profession experienced dramatic growth and went through dynamic evolution, as mentioned earlier.

In 1990, industry icon Gwen Fletcher, the then President of the International Association of Financial Planning (IAFP), signed a deal to bring the Certified Financial Planner (CFP) professional designation to Australia. In 1992, IAFP merged with the Australian Society of Investment and Financial

Advisers (ASIFA) to form the Financial Planning Association of Australia (FPA), which developed a diploma education program in conjunction with Deakin University, which was the entry point to the CFP professional program. The organisation also developed its first Code of Professional Ethics and Practising Standards.

I was a member of the IAFP and fairly active in communicating with other like-minded colleagues in the development of the profession. I then became involved with the FPA and was elected to the Victorian Chapter Committee as the representative of Principal members. I was also chair of the Victorian Principals Committee, representing small business owners. Although I was appointed as the 'Principal' representative, which generally referred to business owners and included major institutions, it was a bit of a misnomer as my interest was focused on professional standards and supporting small business owners. The big end of town had no interest in engaging at the grassroots level and still purported to control the industry.

Principal representatives from each state met regularly at a national level at what was referred to as the National Principals Forum. This forum also included some representatives from major institutions. The divide between the interests of the major institutions and those of the principal representatives and individual practitioners became toxic and confrontational.

The rapid increase in education and professional standards became an issue for the large financial institutions, and they attempted to bully the FPA into appointing an advisory committee to the board consisting of institutional members. In other words, they wanted to control the FPA agenda and head off the drive towards professionalism and the power of the small practice owners and individual practitioners who wanted to develop the profession. As it happened, I had become a major player in this battle, perhaps because of my corporate background or just that I was happy to take up the fight. I was fortunate to gain the support of a few major leaders who could see the benefits of developing the profession. In 1994, this sparked an all-in brawl, in which I was heavily involved, which almost destroyed the FPA. In the end, a working party was established to broker a solution, and eventually an agreement was reached giving principals and advisers representation on the board, together with other elected members who were invariably practitioners. This effectively enabled the FPA to proceed down the professionalism route, and the influence of the major institutions gradually dissipated.

The new governance structure really gave weight to the practitioners and small business owners, who were also practitioners. The large institutions began to struggle with the increasing requirement for standards, and whilst the regulatory standard was not high, more practitioners were acquiring the CFP standard and demanding to be recognised and supported by their licensee principals.

I was appointed to the FPA board after the compromise was reached in 1995. I was also chair of the National Principals Forum, which became active in representing small principals' issues, and we ran conferences offering professional development opportunities. It was a time of rapid change and continuing conflict with various interest groups. Practicing standards, education standards and ethical behaviour were the main drivers. I was appointed chair of the FPA in 2000 and was also fortunate to have been awarded life membership of the FPA.

My time on the FPA board was exciting, and we achieved a great deal in pushing the improvement of education standards and the FPA's role in overseeing the standards of advice of its members, introducing a robust disciplinary program and establishing the Financial Services Complaints Resolution Scheme (FSCRS). The FSCRS was established as a standalone independent arbitrator for consumer complaints and compensation. Whilst the FPA created it and financed it with member funds, it operated completely independent of FPA influence. This was an outstanding initiative first announced by former FPA President Bernie Walsh in 1993 and for which, to my knowledge, the FPA has never received an ounce of recognition by the government or the regulator. The FSCRS has now morphed into the Australian Financial Complaints Authority (AFCA).

Surprisingly, there was constant conflict between both the financial planning profession and the regulator, who continually rejected our suggestions to lift the regulatory education standard to a reasonable level. During my time on the FPA board, we would meet regularly with the ASIC Commissioner and his/her board. We constantly brought up the issue of education standards and industry practices that we felt were at best questionable. The education issue was routinely brushed aside as a matter for the deputy treasurer; they expressed concern about issues we raised, but seemingly did nothing further. It was very frustrating and an indictment on the regulatory process.

Whilst Australia has long been acknowledged as having one of the best financial services regulatory regimes in the world, it has always been compromised by its product focus and its 'one-size-fits-all' nature. The regulation is based on the provision of advice or promotion of any type of financial product and is applicable to anyone, from a highly qualified professional adviser giving complex advice to a telephone call centre operator answering simple customer enquiries. There was always going to be resistance by major institutions who did not want to be forced into complying with a higher education requirement for people giving random product advice. But the problem then arises that the education requirement for giving complex financial advice is compromised.

Despite the FPA's efforts to drive change, the lobbyists working for the big end of town in Canberra convinced politicians that the standards were adequate and the compliance safeguards were in place.

For the next 25 years, there were a raft of scandals and bad behaviours shown by financial advisers and particularly large institutions. Whilst these did trigger some government reviews, the outcomes were compromised by vested interests and their influence over government. It was frustrating, to say the least.

It was 1994 when the FPA first recommended to the government that a diploma level qualification for financial advice should be introduced and has since continually called for a tertiary-based qualification. The FPA introduced a compulsory degree-based education requirement for its membership in 2010.

The FPA had done a fabulous job in driving up professional standards within its membership realm of influence over 30 years. However, whilst the government and the regulator had a habit of criticising the industry for its constant failings, it refused to embrace the standards the professional body was espousing and that there were serious problems in the broad advice arena.

It was not until the 2018 Hayne Royal Commission into the Misconduct in the Banking, Superannuation and Financial Services Industry exposed outrageous behaviour by the major institutions and rogue advisers that real reform finally occurred. That included a lifting of the education to a bachelor's degree standard, the introduction of compulsory knowledge and ethics exams for advisers and various regulatory changes relative to compliance. Several major institutions were issued with enormous fines and financial sanctions.

Our decision to establish our graduate mentoring program in 1995 put us in good stead to not only fight for the increase in professional standards, but when the regulatory education standards were finally uplifted to a degree base,, our advisers were already compliant and in fact still exceeded the minimum standard. But the industry at large did not meet these standards, and there was a massive departure of advisers who were unwilling to undertake higher level education, thus causing a shortage of professional advisers.

My meeting with the prime minister

In 2001, when I was chair of the FPA, the government of the day introduced legislation called the Alienation of Personal Services Income. This called for the regulation of personal services income being diverted via tax-effective structures, thus reducing the tax payable. Unfortunately, the regulation had unintended consequences, affecting various professions due to structural issues. For example, doctors who bulk-billed their patients via Medicare were categorised as being employed by Medicare, and therefore their income was taxed at marginal rates even though the doctors were employed by a medical practice, usually via a service trust.

In the case of financial planners, who practiced under the authority of a securities dealer licensee, a similar problem occurred. If they were rewarded through product-based commissions, these were paid to the licensee and then disbursed to the adviser. Even though the adviser was employed by their own corporate entity, they were categorised as employees of the licensee who were obliged to tax them as employees and retain tax at personal marginal rates.

The government had recognised this issue when it was raised by the medical profession and granted them an exclusion. But after attempting on several occasions to achieve a similar outcome for financial advisers, we were met with a closed door by the then Treasurer Peter Costello. This issue would be disastrous for the industry as a whole and had to be resolved.

I attended a charity dinner hosted by the then Assistant Treasurer David Kemp and sat on his table accompanied by industry leaders who were similarly affected. I was elected by the group to tackle the assistant treasurer and obtain an agreement from him to act, which I did. He promised to get back to me by the following Thursday, but that phone call never came.

I was furious. As I was to chair a conference of CFP members in Sydney the following week, I decided to write an extremely aggressive opening address that attacked the government and included an ultimatum to the then Prime Minister, John Howard, that if he did not act, we would throw the weight of our members and their networks against his party at the forthcoming federal elections.

I sent a draft of my speech to the FPA's public relations manager to neaten up for me. Unbeknown to me, she sent a copy to the prime minister's press secretary. Just before I went on stage to deliver my speech, I had a call from the public relations manager to say she had received a message from the prime minister's office requesting that I meet with him the following week. As a result, I was able to deliver my speech and then announce to the audience that the prime minister had agreed to meet with us. It was a very emotional moment.

I met with the prime minister and explained the situation. To his great credit, he had done his homework, challenged our position, and then agreed to investigate. He said that if what I had told him was correct, he would act to change the regulation.

The following is an extract from *Money Management Magazine* (Engel 2001[2]).

FPA attacks Government and ATO

Financial Planning Association (FPA) chairman John Hewison has blasted the Federal Government and the Australian Tax Office (ATO) over their stance on alienation of personal services income.

Hewison told today's CFP conference the interpretation of the alienation legislation by the ATO was "completely ludicrous and unjust".

"As is the reputation of the regime of the current taxation commissioner, justice and fair play being not virtues to which it aspires," he said.

"In fact, our experience in dealing with representatives of the ATO have been characterised by a mood of arrogance and total lack of concern."

Hewison will meet with Prime Minister John Howard next week to voice the financial planning industry's concerns personally.

After my meeting with the prime minister, he agreed with our submission and implemented a change to the legislation.

---

2   Engel S (4 May 2001) 'FPA attacks Government and ATO', *Money Management* Magazine, accessed 19 July 2024. Reproduced with permission.

The international scene

As mentioned earlier, the FPA had become licensed to offer the Certified Financial Planner (CFP) professional designation in Australia from 1992. The CFP professional mark was created in the US and then marketed internationally. Early adopters were Australia, Canada and Japan, followed by many other countries, including the United Kingdom, Germany, South Africa and Hong Kong. Today there are 27 affiliate countries that have adopted the standard. Representatives from each international affiliate formed the International CFP Council, which met twice a year to discuss the development of standards and the reach of the brand internationally. The agenda was controlled by the US, which was suffocating and inappropriate as it was very much US-focused and had little interest in the international side. In 2004, following a sustained campaign led by Australia and Canada, the international CFP professional marks were purchased by the newly formed Financial Planning Standards Board (FPSB), giving the international affiliates control outside of the US. My friend and colleague Ray Griffin was appointed as the inaugural chair of the FPSB board of directors.

I was one of three people who represented Australia on the International CFP Council from 1999 to 2004, when the FPSB was formed. I was then elected to the FPSB board of directors from 2004 to 2007. Unfortunately, I chose to resign mid-term due to my father's terminal illness.

It is reasonable to say that Australia was a leader on the international stage and was at the forefront of standard setting. It was an extremely exciting time, and I enjoyed the experience of comradeship with international colleagues from 20 countries around the world in setting universal professional education and practicing standards.

As I look back over my experiences with the FPA and the financial planning profession generally, I have massive admiration for those of us who pioneered the drive to professionalism and those who continued to drive the profession to its ultimate transition to a degree-based profession. I have particular regard for former FPA chair Matthew Rowe and CEO Mark Rantall, who both had the courage to transition the FPA to a practitioner-only professional association in 2011. It is difficult to believe that it took so long to finally convince those responsible for protecting the public interest to listen to what the FPA had been telling them for over 30 years. Ultimately, it was massive institutional non-compliance and illegal conduct causing widespread damage to consumers that brought about change.

I have been fortunate enough to have been involved at a momentous time in the evolution of the financial planning profession in Australia and globally. I take great pride in what I and my colleagues achieved over the years and huge satisfaction in the recreation of a true profession.

Chapter 20

Distilling our values

Fun, family, empowerment and excellence

At our team retreat in 2018, shortly after I stepped down as managing director, which was attended by around 40 of our team members, we ran a session with the objective to find what best described our business in just four words.

Attendees were asked to write words down on sticky notes that they felt described our business. Each then came up and placed the notes on a whiteboard, with any words that were of a similar meaning being placed on top of each other.

The first thing that amazed me were the number of notes each person had written but also how many people had written the same words or similar, which indicated that everyone at the table had a great understanding of the values of the business and were like-minded in their opinion of what that represented.

We then distilled the words to determine which were similar in meaning, and then chose the word that best described that particular quality until we had just four words: fun, family, empowerment and excellence.

I will briefly explain how we came to this outcome.

Fun

As I mentioned earlier, I always had a desire to create a business where people would enjoy their working life, not see it as just another job. This was the word chosen by the group to describe the atmosphere where we worked and the close relationship we enjoyed together. It also described the camaraderie and the nature of the relationships we enjoyed with our clients and our other colleagues. Fun also described what our clients experienced in their relationships with us.

It is a little hard to imagine that a business involved in the serious field of financial strategy advice and managing money could be a fun place to be! No doubt culture had a lot to do with it, but maybe it's the focus on relationships and achieving outcomes that makes it what it is. We are essentially a people business, and the technical stuff is a matter of fact.

Family

Family describes the relationships we enjoy and the genuine care we show for each other in the workplace and personally. It also described the relationship we shared with our clients, who we considered to be part of our family, and the way they related to us.

Financial planning and management is a very intimate business, and as a result, we develop very close relationships with clients looking after their financial affairs. We emphasise the need for building a caring and trusted relationship, and most clients become just like family.

When clients visited our office, it was a bit like a family reunion with lots of hugging, laughing and chatter. It is not unusual to see a group of our team and clients crowd around the reception area or in the amenities space, enjoying a catch-up. The clients just love it and so do our people.

Empowerment

Empowerment of our people is the linchpin of our organisation. But likewise, the empowerment our clients achieved through the confidence they derived from their relationship with us was a vital cog. The fact that the group recognised and acknowledged the importance of the empowerment piece was very satisfying to me.

Excellence

We are obsessed with the achievement of excellence in everything we do. The professional standards we set for ourselves, the systems we develop, the quality of our relationships, the work that we do, and the outcomes we achieve. And a lot of that comes down to the culture in which we live and the collective pride in what we want to achieve.

This exercise was surprisingly powerful, as it demonstrated emphatically that our team all had buy-in and were on the same page of understanding the values we shared and our ultimate mission. Concentrating the focus into four words only served to sharpen that understanding and our culture. These four words feature prominently in our staff amenities area and maintain our awareness of our reason for being.

When I have shared this with clients, they absolutely get it. They have expressed that this also describes their experience with us, which is an added bonus.

Mission accomplished

After stepping out of the managing director role, I worked in a part-time capacity for a time, initially looking after my close long-term clients and mentoring the associate advisers whilst chairing the board. I gradually reduced this work and finally retired altogether in 2023. We still retain a small shareholding in the business, but I am not involved directly in its operation. It was easy for me to step down and walk away, as it was always in the plan. My son assuming the role of managing director, however, was an unexpected surprise. I must admit that having a father-son, chair and managing director relationship was not always easy, so I am happy to now just be his dad.

I deliberately stayed away from the office to clear the way for Andrew to develop in his new role. In retrospect, I regret stepping into the chair role, and if I had my time again, I would have recommended the appointment of an external chair following Rob Robert's retirement. The company now has an external chair and is moving towards a non-executive board, which, with the benefit of hindsight, we should have done earlier.

As I look back on my career experience, I am absolutely blown away by what we have achieved. I have fulfilled all my core beliefs and strategic outcomes in ways that I could never have imagined. I had no preconceived idea at how big we would grow and how long we would have endured. But at the time of writing, we are about to celebrate our 40th anniversary in 2025 and are still going strong.

As I reflect on my original dream to create a professional business, I am extraordinarily proud of what we have accomplished. What I could not have anticipated is the extent of our accomplishments along the way and the quality people who have emerged and flourished through their involvement.

When I think about my core beliefs and now see how powerful the outcomes have been, I find it hard to believe what my team and I have achieved. It is all centred around standards and empowerment, a commitment to excellence and innovation, and the courage to embrace and pioneer change. Then succession planning has been vital to our facilitating and achieving longevity.

The other important ingredient has been our wonderful client relationships, of which many have become my lifelong friends. Likewise, our professional relationships have been incredible, and I remain in touch with many of them as well.

It would be remiss of me to pretend that there have not been disagreements and arguments along the way, which is just a fact of life in any business, and there have been disappointments. I have got plenty of scars from my experiences, but I have no regrets. Sure, I have made mistakes and could have done things better, but I figure it is better to have a go and get it wrong than not doing anything at all.

My journey has been exhilarating and rewarding but punctuated by almost unbelievable and heartbreaking challenges that could have broken me and ruined us. But we survived and benefitted from the experiences by learning from the negatives and turning them into positives through innovation and our determination to succeed in the face of adversity. Finally, I have achieved all I set out to achieve at the start, but to the extent and in ways that I could never have imagined in my wildest dreams. I am humbled by what we have achieved as a group and the legacy that now exists.

The business, now operating as Hewison Private Wealth, has eight equity partners with plans to appoint others in the foreseeable future. It manages over $2 billion of client funds with an annual revenue of well over $20 million and growing. It employs a team of over 50 people, including 11 professional advisers and eight associate advisers.

I am proud and privileged to say that we have truly created a business built to last.

Chapter 21

40 years and still counting

40th anniversary celebrations

As I write this, we have recently celebrated our 40th anniversary
with a cocktail party at a beautiful venue by Albert Park Lake, just
outside the Melbourne CBD. Preparations had been underway
for some months, led by HPW Head of Marketing Creina Lister,
with input from MD Andrew Hewison and other members of the
HPW team, including some contributions from me.

In preparation for the event, Creina had arranged several
video interviews and overviews in which I participated. However,
Helen and I were unclear about the details of the function, aside
from my role as one of the speakers.

As the date grew closer, Creina sent me an email with the
invitation list attached and asked me to review it beforehand,
adding anyone I wanted included. As I opened the attachment,
I was amazed to see that around 400 people were on the
invitation list. Professional associates, the entire HPW team
and, of course, many of the firm's clients. Suddenly, it dawned
on me that this was going to be far grander than I had
imagined.

Finally, the date arrived, and we drove to the venue, where
the car park was packed and people were everywhere. As Helen
and I walked through the front entrance, we were confronted
by hundreds of smartly dressed people and the wave of noise

from enthusiastic conversation. Then we were surrounded by familiar people wanting to say hello and chat, and by clients I had never met who wanted to introduce themselves and discuss their experience with the firm. It was a wonderful experience, unlike anything we had ever encountered.

As the formal part of the evening began, Creina's video started proceedings on a massive screen. It was incredible and captured all the qualities and ambitions we had endeavoured to achieve throughout our 40 years of existence. It featured images from over the years, which brought back some wonderful memories but also reflected our family culture and the standards we consistently aimed to achieve. Many of the HPW team featured, along with some of our clients. I was utterly blown away by the consistency of the messages that came through – values, standards, independence, client-first focus, relationships and family – in fact, all of the core values I have talked about in this book. The passion with which the clients spoke about the firm and its people brought tears to my eyes.

HPW independent Chairman Adrian Hondros, a man with broad experience in the financial services sector, opened the speeches with his reflections on how HPW was unique in the financial planning profession and one of the few that could truly be called independent. He also spoke of the quality of the HPW team and its commitment to client-focused advice.

I have to confess that I am a highly emotional individual, so by this time, I was overwhelmed as I climbed on stage to deliver my speech. I managed to fumble my way through talking about our start, our core beliefs, and my pride in having not only achieved all these values but also in having them continue and strengthen beyond my involvement.

Me with HPW
Chairman Adrian
Hondros and MD
Andrew Hewison

Recounting the journey over 40 years to an audience of clients,
professional colleagues and the HPW team

An enthusiastic gathering of around 400 members of the HPW 'family' overlooking Albert Park Lake and the Melbourne skyline

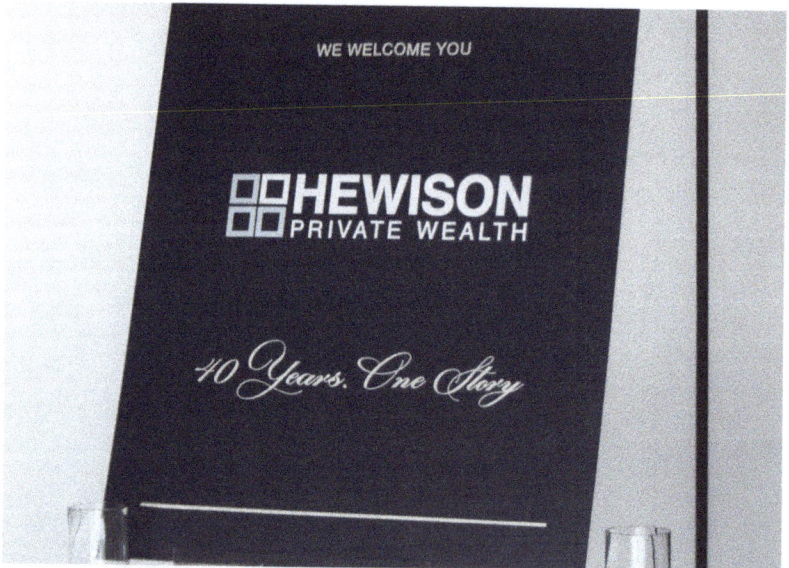

Our 40-year celebration theme – 40 years of consistent standards and client-first philosophy that has stood the test of time and built everlasting relationships

My son and Managing Director Andrew closed the formal part of the night with a stirring speech about how internal values and individual empowerment remain key strategies, and how the family's sense of belonging has been retained despite the company's growth. Throughout the speeches, I looked at the audience and saw continuous nodding as a sign of approval for the points the speakers made.

After the formal presentations, I was kept very busy with clients approaching me to tell stories about how their families were all 'Hewison' clients and how much they enjoyed and were grateful for the relationships. I spoke with relatives of past clients who had passed, and they told me how much they valued their relationships with me and the team. It went on for some time, which was so humbling, yet fulfilling and far beyond any expectations I had.

I always knew we had built something special in our people, our values, and our client relationships, which are more like an extended family than an adviser/client relationship. But I had never imagined just how astonishingly close and personal they were. I always considered my clients my friends, and many of them became lifelong close friends. However, I didn't realise that this was universal across the entire client base, nor did I realise the significance of these relationships to people's lives. Extraordinary!

I have noted my feelings of pride and gratitude for my teammates elsewhere in this book. Still, my gratitude has grown to a new level, and I take great joy in knowing they are living the dream, gaining personal satisfaction from their accomplishments and enjoying the journey together in a fun, family atmosphere.

Thanks, Robert Townsend, for your book *Up the Organisation*, which introduced me to the power of empowerment all those decades ago. That is the basis of the culture we have been able to create, and my colleagues continue to drive forward in an atmosphere of excitement and enthusiasm to be the best of the best, deliver superior client outcomes, and have fun doing it.

As I close this final chapter, I am overcome with feelings of pride, gratitude, satisfaction and fulfilment at our accomplishments and the great work we have done in looking after people's financial wellbeing, partnering in their personal financial empowerment, and helping them achieve their hopes and dreams. However, the personal relationships are by far the most rewarding part of the journey.

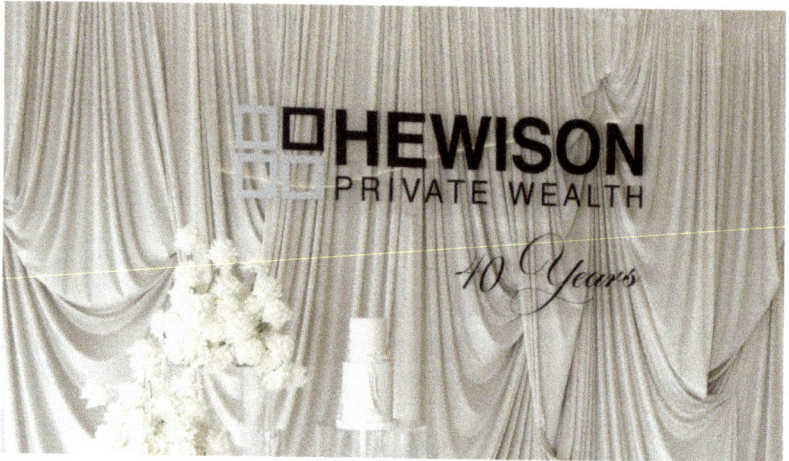

40 years in the making and looking forward
to the next exciting 40 years